W9-CMI-880

MISTAKE
IT LIKE A
MAN

DAVE MEURER

Multnomah® Publishers *Sisters, Oregon*

MISTAKE IT LIKE A MAN
published by Multnomah Publishers, Inc.

© 2006 by Dave Meurer
International Standard Book Number: 1-59052-744-5

Cover photo by Steve Gardner, www.shootpw.com

Unless otherwise indicated, Scripture quotations are from:
The Holy Bible, New International Version (NIV)
© 1973, 1984 by International Bible Society,
used by permission of Zondervan Publishing House
Other Scripture quotations are from:
The Holy Bible, *English Standard Version* (ESV)
© 2001 by Crossway Bibles, a division of Good News Publishers.
Used by permission. All rights reserved.
The Holy Bible, King James Version (KJV)

Multnomah is a trademark of Multnomah Publishers, Inc.,
and is registered in the U.S. Patent and Trademark Office.
The colophon is a trademark of Multnomah Publishers, Inc.

Printed in the United States of America

For information:
MULTNOMAH PUBLISHERS, INC.
601 N. LARCH ST.
SISTERS, OREGON 97759

Library of Congress Cataloging-in-Publication Data
Meurer, Dave, 1958-
Mistake it like a man : an imperfect guy's guide to romance, kids, and Secret
Service motorcades / by Dave Meurer.
    p. cm.
ISBN 1-59052-744-5
1. Christian men—Religious life—Humor. 2. Husbands—Religious life—
Humor. 3. Fathers—Religious life—Humor. I. Title.
BV4528.2.M48 2006
248.8'42—dc22

                              2006009944

06 07 08 09 10—10 9 8 7 6 5 4 3 2 1 0

For Tim Holler
A Wise and Faithful Friend,
A Confidant and Counselor.
I Owe You More Than I Can Ever Repay,
But That Will Not Keep Me From Pointing Out That
I Still Have More Hair Than You.

Contents

PART 1
The Facts of Wife:
A Man and His Marriage

PART 2
Don't Try This at Home:
A Man and His Kids

PART 3
Dude Awakening:
A Man and His Faith…in Today's World

Foreword

Ladies and gents, it's time for you to embark on a journey through the world as Dave Meurer sees it. It's unlike anything else you're likely to experience. This book is like a pair of those goofy 3-D glasses, helping you see the world through the eyes of the funniest, quirkiest person you've ever known. Dave has a unique way of turning even the most mundane moments of life into colossal messes that anyone in his right mind wouldn't have to bother with.

His stories also have an uncanny way of showing you how brilliant his wife Dale is—and how incredibly powerful and gracious God has been to bring those two together. Dave presents her as a sage and himself as the jester, and together they manage the little kingdom God has given them with a mixture of stumbling and grace.

Dave also has another gift to offer you in addition to fits of drink-spilling, side-splintering, "Hey honey, you gotta hear this!" laughter that accompanies every story he shares. It's much more subtle, but it's the true value of this book. As you turn the pages, your laughter will open a window into your spirit and you'll begin to see how Dave's quirky perspective unveils rich wisdom about life, bringing a clarity to the truth and consequence of our decisions that you'll find nowhere else.

Dave's incredible ability to present truth in the rich wrapping of humor gives credence to the idea that laughter can be one of life's greatest teachers. And when you turn the final page of *Mistake It Like a Man,* you'll feel as if Dave's an old friend, as if you've had dinner many times in the Meurer home…and that you've learned a great deal more about yourself and your faith than you ever expected.

Not bad for a humor book.

Enjoy!

— Brian Hedrick
Editor, *Stand Firm* Magazine

Acknowledgments

Right off the bat I need to thank my lovely wife Dale for allowing me to write a lot about our life, and for only rarely utilizing the nuclear veto pen of doom.

My wife is also the calm at the center of the storm. Without her, I'd sink like a brick surfboard.

I thank my two sons, Mark and Brad, for being very good sports year after year, and book after book. I love you both more than you'll ever know. Pizza is on me, guys.

"The gang" (you know who you are) provided a welcome distraction and bouts of silliness and immaturity at just the right time, especially when things were hectic and I really should have been working but I kept checking my e-mail instead. Knock it off!

Steve Laube, my agent, landed this deal with the publisher, so he is legally culpable here. We've been working together for years, so he can't exactly claim to be a clueless and innocent bystander. Anyone who reads my material can legitimately hold Steve responsible. If you need me to testify, I'll be pleased to do so. That's the kind of civic-minded person I am.

PART 1

The Facts of Wife
A Man and His Marriage

It's About Time

In an effort to more efficiently utilize my time, I recently purchased a wireless Bluetooth earpiece that links to my cell phone, thus enabling me to walk down the street conducting "hands-free" conversations while also appearing to suffer from delusions.

Not only does this tiny earpiece increase my productivity, but as an added bonus, complete strangers sometimes stuff a few dollars in my hand and even give me part of their sandwich.

I love this gadget. Sadly, my wife Dale couldn't immediately see the enormous benefits of my new device.

"What's that ridiculous-looking thing stuck on the side of your head, and why is it flashing a blue light? You look like a cyborg," she said, in a manner indicating I needed to reconsider my plans to buy her a matching Bluetooth for her birthday.

"It's a state-of-the-art wireless communication device, my love. Not only can I drive more safely, but I can continue my 'hands-free' conversation anywhere I would normally waste time—the store, the gas station, weddings, you name it. No more unproductive down time for the newly wired me!"

She rolled her eyes—an action which, curiously, often accompanies the announcement of my latest great idea.

"Dave, you already carry around that irritating Blackberry e-mail thing that's constantly buzzing on your belt. Do you have to be working all the time? I can't believe you actually felt compelled to read an e-mail message the last time we went out to dinner. You're so type-A. What you call 'unproductive time' is what everyone else calls 'the rest of your life when you aren't at work.' I don't want all these 'productivity' objects to crowd out the important down time we need. Even Jesus took time out."

I would have offered her some reassuring words, but in the middle of her comments a call had come in on my Bluetooth, so I caught only part of what she said.

---

you'd **think** women would be **more** understanding

"That sounds fine, Darin. Just make sure you send me a hard copy," I replied, making hand motions to Dale so she would understand I was on the phone. She frowned at me, but for crying out loud, a guy can't have two completely different conversations at the same time. You'd think women would be more understanding.

"Okay," I told her at last. "I'm off the phone now. What were you saying?"

"Dave, if you're going to add that thing to your mix of electronic debris, just make sure you don't use it around me. Don't use it in the house. Never, ever take it on a walk with me. When you're with me, you need to *be* with me."

"Okay, okay," I agreed, suddenly realizing this was a big deal to her.

Regrettably, I tend to be forgetful. A few days later I walked in the house still chatting to the Bluetooth as I wrapped up a call. Dale heaved a big sigh. Inasmuch as we had a date to go out to dinner that night, I feared my little slip-up didn't set a particularly positive tone for the evening.

But Dale was unexpectedly understanding.

"Dave, I've been thinking it over. I've decided you're right. We have too much unproductive time, and it's robbing us of the ability to accomplish important tasks."

"Really?" I asked, surprised.

"Oh yes," she replied. "For instance, we fritter away far too much time on romance. We could be sending urgent e-mails, and you could be having even more talks on your blinking little earpiece. I was thinking we should start scheduling our intimate sessions. What's Thanksgiving week looking like for you?"

"This is June!" I yelped.

"I was thinking perhaps sometime in the Fall, as long as nothing else crops up," she mused, flipping through her planner, which had way too many dates marked with a big black X.

"You know," I replied, biting my lip, "I was just thinking I've been too busy lately. All work and no play makes Dave a dull and obnoxious and very repentant boy who has learned a valuable lesson from the dear wife God has given him, because God understands that without your calming influence I become a frantic and maniacal dolt."

When God wants to get my attention, He never calls me on my Bluetooth. But He often speaks to me through my wife.

May I Take Your Order?

Before I got married I had a profoundly inadequate and narrow understanding of how to order food at a restaurant. I labored under the foolish notion that the waiter was supposed to hand you a menu, which you then used to select a dinner that sounded appealing to you, which you then ordered, which you then ate.

But one day I took my bride, Dale, to an Italian place, glanced at the menu, and said, "I think I'll have the Marsala Chicken."

"That's what I was going to order," she said.

"Great minds think alike," I replied.

"But we can't order the same thing!"

"We can't?"

She shook her head. "We need to try different entrees so we can share."

"But we both want Chicken Marsala," I replied.

"And we can both have some. Plus, we can try something adventurous and new. That's one of the best things about eating out," she explained.

"But what if I only want the chicken?"

"Then you would be wrong."

"I would be wrong about what I want to eat?"

"The idea is to *share,*" she said.

"Let me get this straight—I can't go to a restaurant and just order whatever I want?"

"Correct," she replied.

"Is it, like, a law or something? Is it in the code of federal regulations?"

"It's just common sense."

I frowned. "It's common sense to order a dinner you *don't* want when they're serving the dinner you *do* want?"

Dale sighed. "You make it sound so odd."

"Well, how about if we compromise?" I suggested. "Let's both order Chicken Marsala, and we can share with each other."

Dale rolled her eyes. "That's complete nonsense."

The waiter walked up.

"May I take your order?"

"Yes," I said.

"We need a few more minutes," Dale interjected.

"Certainly," he said, casting a disdainful "you rude halfwit" look at me.

"But I was ready!" I whispered at my wife.

She was staring at the menu. "I think you should try the House Specialty," she advised.

"Which is?" I asked.

"Seared filet mignon wrapped in bacon and topped with foie gras."

Hmmmm. A hunk of beef didn't sound too bad. Maybe this sharing thing would work after all.

"What's foie gras?" I inquired.

"An enlarged goose liver, created by force-feeding the bird. It's a delicacy. And the dinner also comes with a warm spinach salad with pine nuts, raspberries, and a mustard honey dressing. The vegetable is peppered asparagus with capers. Doesn't that sound exotic?" she said.

"A mutant goose gizzard?" I whispered. "Exotic? How about 'terrifying?'"

"Let's try it," she said.

"How about if *you* try it, and I have the chicken?"

"Because *I'm* having the chicken," she said. "We've already been through this."

The waiter returned.

"And have we decided?" he asked, flipping open his order pad.

"Yes," Dale said.

"We need a few more minutes," I said.

"And madam would like?" he asked, ignoring me.

"The Chicken Marsala," she said, folding her menu.

"And you, sir?"

"Ditto," I replied.

"He'll have the House Specialty," Dale said.

"Certainly!" the waiter replied, and spun on his heels and vanished before I could object.

"Hon, what can possibly be wrong about ordering something that I *know* from experience I'll enjoy?"

"What's wrong is that you get completely stuck in your ways, you have the same old thing every time, and it gets boring."

All I could think was, it's not being "stuck" if you're there by your own free choice.

"All my friends feel the same way I do," Dale added.

Well, that certainly settled it. If a bunch of women agree on something, then guys can pretty much kiss off any hope of changing things.

So for the past two decades, we've shared dinners and expanded our culinary horizons. I've tried things I would have never otherwise tried, including halibut, veal, and fresh spinach. Sometimes the food was dreadful, but most times I've been pleasantly surprised. All in all, Dale was right. It *has* been fun to try new things.

So it was somewhat of a surprise when I recently took her back to our favorite Italian place and she decided to have exactly what I was having.

"Let me make sure I understand this—I'm having my favorite old predictable Chicken Marsala, and so are you?"

"Yes," she replied. "It just sounds right for today."

"But we always get different things. We've been ordering different entrees for our entire marriage. This is a huge break with tradition," I pointed out.

"You just need to be more flexible," Dale said.

And her friends all agree with her. So who am I to argue?

After twenty-something years of marriage, my wife still surprises me, delights me, and cracks me up.

If your spouse was just like you, life would be much easier in some ways. You wouldn't have to accommodate each other, because you would already agree. But life would indeed become boring and predictable.

I think God took great pleasure in making men and women "so close, yet so far." Take joy in the inherent differences He's built into both of you.

"May you rejoice in the wife of your youth" (Proverbs 5:18).

3

Fill Her Up!

I take great glee in the thrill of driving my car while basking in the warm glow of the little orange warning light telling me I'm low on gas. This light clicks on when I have about an eighth of a tank left. But I like to keep driving until the fuel gauge needle is lying horizontal, hovering right on the big E. Then I keep on driving a few extra miles, fitting in that last run to the grocery store or eking out one additional commute to work.

I picked up this habit from my dad, who was the undisputed master of squeezing every last gasoline molecule out of the tank before pulling into a service station. I remember once when Dad literally set a world record in maximizing his use of the available fuel supply. I was about eight years old, and the entire family was packed into our 1963 Chevy Impala. Dad had been driving for dozens of miles with the needle collapsed flat on the 'Empty' position when he finally decided to get gas.

About two blocks from the Gulf station, the engine began to gasp and sputter. He pumped the gas pedal and spoke words of encouragement to the halting, shuddering car.

"You can do it, baby," he said.

We slogged slowly through the traffic, with the car making jerky attempts to crawl forward—like an exhausted, disoriented marathon runner staggering blindly toward the finish line.

The car was at a mere crawl as the tires encountered the slight rise in the slope of the driveway leading to the pumps. I was afraid we would stall out and roll back into the street. But we had just enough forward motion to slide up the ramp, cross the critical threshold, and catch the slight downward slope as the engine wheezed, panted, and finally croaked. The car moved, sloth-like, right up to the pump…then quit.

Absolutely perfect timing.

I told Dale, "It was so beautiful, such a feat of fuel maximization artistry, that nearly forty years later it still almost brings tears to my eyes."

"That's so weird," she replied.

Dale will simply never understand my viewpoint on this, no matter how many times I try to explain. I even compared it to the way the Grand Canyon takes your breath away. "It's beyond words. It's just a thing of beauty that has to be soaked up," I said.

"That's the strangest thing I've ever heard you say," she answered. "And given all the strange things you've said over the years, that's saying a lot."

She simply wasn't soaking up Dad's accomplishment.

"don't even **think** of trying that with **me** in the car," she said

---

"And don't even think of trying that with me in the car," she added. "If *you* want to get stranded on the side of the road, have fun. But not with me."

Sigh. She utterly misses the point.

It's a matter of productivity. I don't like to make unnecessary trips to the gas station. I think it's inefficient to gas up the car when it still has a quarter of a tank left. After all, if you do that consistently, you'll make numerous extra trips to the gas station throughout the year. Why would I want to expend precious minutes of my mortal existence on an unnecessary and wholly unproductive activity? Indeed, does the Bible itself not tell us to "redeem the time"? Doesn't the book of Proverbs laud wise planning?

But even with logic and the Bible on my side, whenever Dale takes a trip with me, she insists that I make redundant and unrequired stops at the gas station.

"You have less than a quarter of a tank," she said one day as we were departing for a three-hour trip. "Let's fill up before we leave town."

"But if we drive to the next town, the tank will be close to empty and we can fill up there," I noted.

"Dave, it's fifty miles! We could be barely running on fumes by then," she said.

"That's the spirit!" I said, offering her a high five.

She asked me to get gas anyway.

Cutting things close is something I find exhilarating; Dale finds it agitating. I'm comfortable with a very small margin for error; she wants a margin of several square acres.

"But Hon, we can easily make it to the next town," I said.

"You're probably right," she replied, "but I'll feel better if we have a full tank of gas right from the start."

"But precious seconds of our life are ticking away," I reminded her.

"And precious seconds were ticking when you were watching old reruns of *Everybody Loves Raymond,* but that didn't stop you," she said.

"But those were well-spent precious seconds!" I protested. "It was the episode with the chocolate cake."

"Dave, I would just feel better if you filled up the car."

So, I did it her way. I could have pressed the point; I could have used a calculator to prove we would be fine. But this was about a comfort level, and I just needed to defer to her.

I once got a truly great piece of marriage advice from another guy. "Whenever you and your wife disagree," he said, "when you can't see eye to eye even after you hash out the issue, then make an honest attempt to do whatever is in the best interest of your wife."

That paradigm has simplified things tremendously. The issue isn't miles per gallon or extra trips to the gas station. The issue isn't who's right about the math. The issue is loving my spouse enough to do what's in her best interests. And making her a nervous wreck isn't in her best interest.

Plus, if I learn to use this decision-making model in the little things…it will carry over into other things when the stakes are higher.

After all, Jesus always did what was in the best interests of His bride. And He wants us to imitate Him. "Husbands, love your wives, just as Christ loved the church and gave himself up for her" (Ephesians 5:25).

My Cup Runneth Over

I knew getting married meant I would change many things from my single days. But never in a million years would I have remotely anticipated that these changes included which coffee mug I use.

My favorite coffee mug was a large-capacity hunk of pottery adorned with a grinning face. It stared at me in a sheepish manner every morning. I'd owned this mug for years, and I used it almost daily.

I reached for it one morning and Dale said, "Why don't you use a different cup today? How about this one, with the leaf pattern? It's a perfect match for the mood of an October morning."

Perfect match? Mood?

My new bride, the woman I thought I knew pretty well, might have just as well rattled off a few sentences in German or Chinese. I was taken aback. I seriously had zero idea what on earth she was saying. I mean, the words coming out of her mouth were in English, but they seemed to be random phrases jumbled together in a bizarre order with no discernable meaning. I wouldn't have been any more confused if she'd said, "Why don't we toast the joyful carburetor in the lake? How about this one, with the tuna boat and orange shovel? It's perfect for an October giraffe."

"What?" I said.

"We need to use coffee mugs that match the day," she said.

"I'm going to use the one with the scene of the old barn and the field of wheat."

My mind was still racing, trying to understand.

"I was just going to have some coffee," I explained, very slowly.

"Me too. Let's just use the right cups," she replied, pouring the coffee for us.

Right cups?

I had never, ever, in my entire life given any thought whatsoever to the aesthetic relationship any drinking implement might have with the current season. I just grabbed whatever vessel was closest to me and filled it up. If I made any distinction at all, it was about usable volume. If I was really thirsty, I would grab something big. My use of the grinning coffee mug was simply about employing a cup with sufficient girth to hold a big dose of hot caffeine while providing a comfortable grip.

"A mug is a mug," I told Dale. "It's just a conveyance system to get liquid into the body."

"You have soooo much to learn," Dale said, grinning at me. "The right coffee mug helps set the tone for the day. That's why we have a variety to choose from."

It still didn't make sense, but I went along with it because (a) it made no difference to me, (b) I loved her, and (c) it was just so doggoned cute. All these little female quirks and surprises, while a bit odd, were really kind of delightful. And she found it surprising that this little episode made me want to make out with her.

"Right now?" she asked.

"You have sooooo much to learn," I replied.

My beloved was an endless source of fascination. She was so different from me. If I began to set the table for dinner, she would sometimes say, "Oh, let's use the blue and white plates instead."

Honestly, it simply never occurred to me to choose between two sets of dishes. I just reached for whichever plates were on the lowest shelf. But Dale was teaching me about the new world of artistic presentation.

For example, Dale was a major user of fresh parsley. She would sometimes cook with it, but more often she used it simply to set on the plate for a splash of color contrast. And then, after the meal, we would toss it out with the trash.

---

my default position was utilitarian

The whole idea was utterly foreign to me. As a bachelor, I'd never purchased not-for-consumption greenery. (Actually, since I didn't own a bunny, I felt no need to keep *any* green things in the refrigerator.)

Prior to marrying Dale, my default position was utilitarian. I had exactly one houseplant. It was called an "air fern" because it required neither soil nor water. I did manage to keep plenty of air on hand in the apartment, so my air fern thrived.

Dale's default position is artistic. She's a lover of beauty, and so she began infusing all manner of loveliness into our life. She isn't extravagant about it, and she doesn't empty the checkbook to attain it; she's frugal and patient. But she's always making incremental improvements in our home, in our yard, and throughout her sphere of influence.

She recently began taking college classes in floral design, tropical flowers arranging, and houseplant care. So we have a steady stream of beautiful works of floral art flowing into our home these days. We have so many floral arrangements that Dale is giving them to friends and taking them to work, to the delight of her colleagues.

And I totally love it. I tremendously enjoy the imprint of her creative touch. Food actually seems to taste better when it's presented in an elegant fashion. We don't do meals like this all the time, but often enough that it's a built-in part of our life.

When Dale decided to redecorate our bedroom, I was eager to be involved. We agreed to create a tropical theme, and to try doing it on a dime. We shopped for deals, we dickered with store managers for a better price on close-outs and floor models, we went to garage sales, and we created drapes from tropical-print sheets. It was a blast, and we love the final result. It's eye-pleasing and sets a romantic theme. Hey, anything that makes my beloved feel more amorous works for me.

This is about far more than just a difference in our personalities or our backgrounds. I no longer see Dale's longing for all manner of beauty as a female thing, but as a *God* thing.

Dale's love of beauty, her desire to create something visually pleasing, reflects the glory and nature of God. He has a purpose behind everything He creates, but He's not a utilitarian. God isn't sparse when He decorates. In the flower department alone, He crafted so many exquisite varieties in such stunning numbers and color combinations that they boggle the mind. And consider the trees! The exploding colors of the maples, the grace and soaring reach of the redwood, the gnarled and twisted branches of the valley oak—and there are gazillions of others.

In my wife I see the creativity of God. I see it in her personality, in her beauty, in her spirit, and in her joy in all that God has made.

It's one more way in which living with this surprising and very different creature has changed me, made me better, and taught me much about our Creator and Savior.

And now, if I'm brewing an evening cup of tea for Dale, I open the cupboard and pick a cup that I think will match her mood. And if she offers to make tea for me, and I grin at her in a sheepish manner...she already knows what mood I'm in.

We've both learned soooooo much.

5

The People's Choice

After many years of working quietly behind the scenes in the political world, the day finally came when I made the decision to throw my own hat in the ring and make a run for elected office.

I knew it would be a daunting task. I understood the challenges were formidable, and I also knew I would need thick skin to withstand the bruising words that often accompany the pursuit of higher office. But even though I'm a seasoned veteran of the political world, I have to admit I was completely taken aback by the immediacy and ferocity of the negative barrage that followed my public announcement.

"Sheer one hundred percent lunacy! There has never been anyone less suited for that office." That was the exact quote.

Regrettably, the critic was my wife Dale.

"But Hon, this could be my big chance," I replied, hurt.

"You want to run for mayor of *Maui?* Did you happen to notice we live in California?" she said, throwing up her hands. "We visited Maui only once for a week's vacation!"

I chewed my lower lip in a sensitive and compassionate manner. "But that trip made a deep impression. I feel a special kinship with the Mauians. I have a vision for them. It's a vision of me on the beach, sipping chilled guava juice and happily fielding questions from my grateful constituents."

I offered Dale the chance to host a campaign fundraising dinner, but she hadn't yet caught the vision.

"Let me say this slowly so you can understand it," she stated. "WE DON'T LIVE IN MAUI! Got it? You can't run for mayor of someplace you don't live!" Then she added, "If you're doing this just to irritate me, you're succeeding."

Regrettably, public servants are often surrounded by naysayers and pessimists. Fortunately, men of vision—such as Abraham Lincoln—did not allow themselves to be discouraged by what former Vice President Spiro Agnew once aptly called the "nattering nabobs of negativism." Of course, Spiro never said that to his wife.

"Dale," I pleaded, "I need your help to pull this off. If the media senses any lack of support from you, the race is as good as over. Any hint of disapproval from you will be the same as holding up a big sign saying, 'My husband is a gibbering nutcase; vote for the other guy.'"

"Let me jot that down before I forget it," she replied.

"Glad you're on board," I said. "Here's how I see the campaign playing out. First, I need to familiarize myself with the key issues. What do Mauians care about? Are there sufficient waves to meet the surfing demand? Are the beaches too sandy? Is there an export market for poi, possibly by packaging it as a car wax? We need to get inside their heads."

"Someone needs to get inside *your* head," Dale replied.

"Exactly. But that's phase two—the people of Maui do, indeed, need to get to know me, hear my story, and understand why I should be entrusted with leading their small but nonetheless significant nation."

"Maui is an *island*, not a *nation!*" Dale snapped.

---

maybe she could **start** a foundation to prevent **cruelty** to mangoes

---

"Good catch—you get to be my researcher," I said. "Write down 'island, not nation' on a three-by-five card. I can't afford any slips. The press will be merciless. Oh, and you might want to start practicing your spousely beaming. There's nothing quite so heartwarming as the candidate standing next to his supportive and beaming spouse. You'll also need to think up a noncontroversial cause to support. Literacy has already been done. Maybe you can start a foundation to prevent cruelty to mangoes. Aren't mangoes basically like monkeys?"

Dale didn't reply, so I glanced up from my campaign planning documents.

Her left eye had developed that quite unsightly twitch that tends to crop up during my best brainstorms. I think all the excitement I generate sometimes overloads her circuits. I just hoped she would get over it before my kick-off press conference.

"Maybe you need to lei down for awhile," I said. "Get it? 'Lei down'? I'll slip those Maui-type words into my speeches so the Mauians feel like I'm one of them. Want to practice beaming at me?"

Her initial attempt fell woefully short. It was less like beaming and more like grimacing with tooth pain.

"That will need some work," I noted. "For now, let's turn our attention to campaign financing."

"If you so much as touch our checkbook," Dale said, "I'm having you placed in a home for the mentally diminished."

She still was not beaming.

"Hon, we aren't financing this ourselves," I assured her. "We'll raise a bunch of loot from people who share my vision. Then we'll establish our required ninety-day residency in Maui. We'll live in our campaign headquarters, which will be conveniently located in a fashionable beach resort. We can hire a bunch of house servants who can double as a spontaneous uprising of my grassroots support. Any questions so far?"

Dale folded her arms. "Anyone in their right mind will see this is nothing more than a scam to get other people to pay for your extended vacation. What's your campaign slogan, 'The Choice of Lunatics'?"

"I was thinking more along the lines of, 'After Three Months in Maui, Even If Dave Loses, Dave Wins!' It has an upbeat, optimistic air about it."

"I have a better slogan," Dale said. "Dave Had Better Drop This Idiotic Scheme, Or His Wife Will Find Ninety-Nine Different Ways to Make His Life Unpleasant."

It wasn't catchy…but it won anyway.

Hey, try these words of Jesus on for size:

Whoever wants to become great among you must be
your servant, and whoever wants to be first must be
your slave—just as the Son of Man did not come to
be served, but to serve, and to give his life as a ransom
for many.

MATTHEW 20:26–28

Our divine calling—as a spouse, as a parent, as a friend—is
always to serve. If more of us invested time and energy into pon-
dering how we could truly *serve* others, and then carried out
those plans, the world would be such a sweeter place.

It all starts at home. The more we give to and serve our
spouse, the more he or she feels motivated to reciprocate. It's an
endless cycle—in a good way. Divorce would become so much
rarer if we consciously put our mate first.

Jesus wasn't just being poetic when He asserted, "It is more
blessed to give than to receive" (Acts 20:35). As with so many
things Jesus taught, this statement seems counterintuitive. We
think we'll be happy when we get our way. But just try it; put
His words to the test.

In reality, we'll truly be happy when God gets *His* way. So
let God have His way in your life.

May the blessing of God rest on your marriage, for better or
for worse, for richer or for poorer…until death does its part.

The Ten Main Things I Know About Women

News flash! If you eat a steady diet of fast food, you'll gain weight! And your arteries will contain enough grease to lube an entire fleet of Volvos!

This shocking information was revealed in a recent news magazine.

I just love those periodic "studies" that "discover" glaringly obvious facts, such as the fact that a dozen Winchells donuts do not constitute a balanced breakfast (unless you have an even mix of chocolate and maple).

Here's another breakthrough finding: Men and women are *different!*

Isn't that astonishing news?

How many male laboratory rats were driven insane by forced exposure to Oprah TV shows before the researchers deduced that "male" and "female" are, in fact, different genders with different interests?

In an effort to provide you with some truly useful information, with no taxpayer funding involved, I hereby submit to you my own findings based on more than two decades of empirical research involving my wife.

Here are the ten main things I know about women:

ONE: Women are permitted to make impulse purchases, and men are not.

Women can go to a craft fair and buy an artsy item to hang

on the wall—say, a wooden Uncle Sam sculpted from a weathered fence rail—even though that item was never on any shopping list. However, if a guy makes an impulse purchase of an item that would be perfect for one of his colleagues at the office—for example, a charming rustic sign that reads, "Your village called; their idiot is missing"—his wife will mutter something about "flushing money down the toilet." And if a husband makes a further impulse purchase later that week, such as a new Chrysler PT Cruiser, his wife will quite often become downright snippy.

Furthermore, for some reason these male shopping whims tend to make your spouse less romantically inclined for at least a couple of days, even if the PT Cruiser has an exceptional stereo system and, after all, she always said she *likes* music.

So avoid impulse purchases.

TWO: Even if it's really, really hot outside, and even if your kids completely agree with your proposed solution, your wife will probably not agree with your idea to charge a boat on your Visa card.

THREE: When it comes to sex, men are quickly aroused and can easily block out distractions, but women are risk-averse and overly concerned about peripheral details.

For example, if a guy is sitting next to his wife and he pulls her close and whispers in her ear, "Give me one reason I shouldn't make passionate love to you at this moment," his wife will likely reply, "Well, for starters, this traffic light is going to change any minute."

FOUR: If you do the dishes, your wife will inexplicably find you irresistibly cute and will want to make out with you. This is so odd. I suspect that when the people at the Palmolive research lab created their "new and improved" dishwashing soap, they loaded it up with pheromones.

FIVE: While men enjoy normal movies involving submarines and explosions and daring rescues, women prefer movies that involve British actors and shrubbery and agonizingly slow plots. And they want *you* to watch these movies with them. The only benefit to these movies is that your spouse will be all weepy and emotional and want to be hugged. This can lead to a romantic interlude, as long as you can avoid slipping into a shrubbery-induced coma before the movie's over.

as she reached for it, my blood ran cold

Thoughtful husband that I am, I recently agreed to watch one of those movies with my wife. But as she reached for it, my blood ran cold. The box wasn't some thin little case; it was a thick, book-like holder that pretty much screamed "miniseries!"

Three hours and forty-five minutes later, I paused the movie, turned to my wife and said, "Hon, when does the plot actually start?" Oh, there had been plenty of things happening all right—waltzes, tea parties, crumpets, horseback rides across verdant green fields for no apparent reason, droll comments, more waltzes, mansions, and for excitement, more horseback rides. But nothing that could actually be called a plot. I was slipping into the dreaded coma. My wife, on the other hand, was deeply touched by the story, and had tears in her eyes.

We're only halfway through the series. Pray for me.

SIX: Your wife's definition of "going out on a date" does not include anything that involves fish guts, target shooting, or screaming helpful vision improvement tips at an umpire.

SEVEN: If your wife reluctantly agrees to go to an air show with you, and one of the main events involves a helicopter dropping an Oldsmobile several hundred feet onto the tarmac in a metal-crushing, glass-smashing spectacle of awesome destruction, your wife will look at you and say, "I don't get it."

When you attempt to explain why it was one of the coolest things you've ever seen, and how you would give your right nostril to see them drop a Hummer, especially if it burst into flame on impact, and how your dream job would be piloting the helicopter that dropped vehicles to the unyielding pavement, your wife will reply, "I still don't get it."

Then she'll say you owe her three movies involving British actors and shrubbery. At this point, it's okay to weep.

EIGHT: Although women say they crave spontaneity and little surprises, if you try to accommodate that desire by jumping out of the closet and yelling "boo," you can usually regain most of your limb function after a few months of physical therapy.

NINE: It's precisely because women are so different from men that men cannot help but be fundamentally changed by the day-in, day-out experience of living with this utterly wonderful, bewildering, fascinating creature whom God tells us to love with the very passion and commitment Christ bestows on the church. Living with my wife has required me to sacrifice, to change, to take huge emotional risks, and to utterly commit myself to another human being. In short, she's the major means by which God is building Christlikeness into my character.

TEN: As you get older, your wife will insist that you have

annual prostate exams. She'll say this is because she loves you and doesn't want you to take risks with your health, but I think it's simply retaliation for childbirth.

Let the Blames Begin!

One of the big advantages of marriage is the security of knowing that, come what may in this uncertain world, you always have a partner you can blame.

Blame is a marital perk that ranks right up there with sex, and considering the fact that the average guy can perform blame multiple times in a single day, and even several times per hour after building up his stamina, blame is arguably even better than sex.

Go ahead and admit it. Blame makes us feel good, which is why we do it. Blame is a great way to relieve tension. We can be feeling all surly and grouchy, perhaps not even knowing why, and we find sweet release in blaming our wife, or the kids, or co-workers, or the state legislature, or the dog, or the Chicago Bears.

Blaming someone else is an inherent part of what it means to be a guy. It comes naturally, so please don't think I'm blaming you for it. Nor am I lecturing you about it. I engage in blame all the time, so I'm the last one to point fingers.

While a lot of sermons imply that blame is immoral or shallow, I feel we should embrace and even celebrate blame. Indeed,

I think we can make a strong theological case that blame is quite biblical. While many ministers focus excessively on rather heavy topics like sanctification, which require all kinds of self-discipline and other puritanical virtues, most Christian scholars have given insufficient attention to the cheery doctrine of blamification, which is way easier to implement.

Before anyone gets offended or accuses me of heresy, answer the following two questions:

(1) Did Adam and Eve blame others for the mess in which they found themselves?

(2) Is the account of this blame-fest found in the Bible?

If the answer to these two questions is yes, does it not then follow that if blame is found in the Bible, blame is biblical?

I rest my case. (And I never even went to seminary.)

---

blame keeps me from being introspective

In addition to being biblical, I find that blame helps keep me from becoming introspective and brooding about my faults.

For example, during my recent annual physical exam, my doctor noticed I weighed as much as a Volvo station wagon, and he got all testy and critical. I was beginning to slip into the unwelcome pit of guilt, but the portly steed of blame staggered to the rescue.

DOCTOR: "Dave, your test results were, once again, awful. Your blood sugar level places you at the 'borderline diabetic' level, your weight is a risk factor for heart disease, and you're clearly not engaging in thirty minutes per day of aerobic exercise. We've had this identical conversation every year for the past five years, and you never change any of your behaviors. I'm going to be blunt here, Dave. The blame lies solely with you."

ME: "Not so fast, Doc. My wife happens to be an excellent cook, and she makes these completely killer chocolate chip cookies that are, quite literally, impossible to resist. I can easily scarf down a dozen in a single session. Were it not for her culinary skills, I could easily be mistaken for an Olympic diver. So she's legally culpable here. I think a jury of my peers would agree she needs to be held accountable for her reckless endangerment of my health."

The doctor not only glared at me, but he was unusually aggressive during the prostate exam. And I don't for a moment believe his explanation that current medical protocols require the use of a small, greased jackhammer.

I was so traumatized by his acrimonious comments and unkind actions that I felt compelled to seek comfort at a local ice cream parlor.

When you think about it, since God is the one who created women, and women happen to be the most frequent purveyors of dessert items, we may even need to consider whether true blame should be traced back to heaven.

Although this line of argumentation wasn't terribly effective for Adam, and although it got him tossed out of the Garden of Eden, and although it plunged humanity into moral and physical decay…this drawback doesn't detract from the brilliance of his defense. It merely gives us someone else to blame: Adam!

I hope you've found these words helpful. But if not, don't blame me!

The Curious Case of the
Missing Spectacles

The onset of my wife's condition was so subtle that I completely missed it. Looking back, there were numerous tell-tale signs, but they were such little things that I chalked them up to simple mistakes or absentmindedness. Besides, we were only in our forties, so it didn't occur to me that something more serious could be going on.

Then one day my glasses vanished.

"Dale, where did you put my glasses?" I asked.

"You misplaced them *again*?" she responded. "Did you backtrack to where you last had them?"

"They were right here," I said, pointing to the small table near the couch. I always left my glasses in the same place *precisely* to avoid having to look for them. It was an immutable habit.

"Well," Dale said, "you got home pretty late last night from your meeting. Maybe you left them in the car."

"No, they were exactly right here," I retorted, placing my finger on the very place I'd laid them.

"Go check the car anyway," she said.

I breathed a deep sigh. "Dale, there would have been no reason, no reason at all, for me to pull into the driveway, take off my glasses, and walk into the house without them," I said.

"Go look anyway," she said. "The last time this happened, you insisted they were not in the car, and I tore the house apart looking for them. Then lo and behold, they were on the back-seat of your car right where you left them."

"That was completely different," I replied. "That was during the day, so I was wearing my prescription sunglasses. I placed my regular glasses in the back seat for safekeeping. But last night I was wearing my regular glasses, so I would have walked into the house wearing them."

"Go outside and look anyway," Dale said.

"But Hon, it would be a ridiculous waste of—"

"Go outside and look anyway," she said again, as though she didn't realize she'd just uttered those exact words mere moments earlier. Hmmm. A disturbing sign, for sure.

"But, my sweet, as I was trying to say…"

"GO OUTSIDE AND LOOK ANYWAY," she said in a much louder tone, almost as though she were suffering from a dramatic hearing impairment.

To humor her, I decided to go outside and go through the motions of looking. I also took my cell phone so I could place a furtive call to our family doctor and inform him of Dale's strange symptoms.

I opened the car door and was stunned to find my glasses on the front passenger seat. I stared for a full ten seconds as the magnitude of the situation hit home. It was all immediately clear. Glaringly, painfully clear. Obviously, Dale must have taken my glasses from the table late last night and placed them in my car.

I walked hesitantly back into the house. Dale was in the kitchen, out of eyesight.

"They were there, weren't they?" she called out.

How could she have known this unless she placed them

there? What else but a tragic medical condition or severe psychological dysfunction could explain her bizarre actions?

Joining her in the kitchen, I decided to steer the conversation gently so as not to push her over the brink in her delicate condition.

"Yes, the glasses were there. What do you make of this curious circumstance?" I asked.

"There's nothing curious about it," she replied, placing a teabag in a cup of hot water. "I watch you do it all the time. You pull into the driveway, take off your glasses, rub the bridge of your nose, and either put your glasses in your pocket or set them down in the car. You just forgot what you did. Mystery solved."

Ahhhh. Projection *and* denial. This was more serious than I thought.

I decided to drop the matter and just contact a medical expert within the week.

Regrettably, before I could follow up with a doctor the crisis was repeated. On another morning, I couldn't find my glasses anywhere. I was tearing through the house, looking under furniture, peeking in cupboards, and opening refrigerator crisper drawers, when Dale asked what I was doing.

"Well, my glasses seem to have disappeared," I said.

"Oh, no. Not again," Dale said. "This is beginning to get alarming."

"I'm glad you agree," I replied, relieved that she was coming to grips with her condition.

"Just wear your old pair or you'll be late for work," Dale said.

I glanced at my watch. She was right. I needed to run. I

snatched my old glasses out of my office desk drawer and ran out the door.

It was a good thing I had the back-up pair. Without my glasses, I have to resort to driving with the guidance afforded by those "Braille bumps" the highway department has thoughtfully placed on the freeway to aid visually impaired motorists. But this driving technique requires a lot of weaving, which often gets the highway patrol people all pushed out of shape. I can barely get five miles down the road before they pull me over again. You'd think they would learn after a while.

---

you'd **think** they would **learn** after a while

Two days later, my back-up spectacles also vanished. I dared not tell Dale. I didn't feel equipped to break the news to her on my own. There was no telling what she might do in her fragile state.

"Dale, isn't it time for your annual physical exam?" I asked casually.

"No. And why are you watching the news with your sun-glasses on?" she asked.

"Boy, have you noticed how bright the television screen has been lately?" I replied.

Dale folded her arms. "Don't tell me your old glasses are gone too. Please don't tell me that."

"Well, I hate to break this to you, but I placed them very carefully right on the table next to the…"

"No, you didn't," she interrupted. "Your glasses didn't sprout tiny legs and wander away, they weren't abducted by aliens, we weren't visited by a burglar who specializes in ripping off old glasses with horribly outdated frames, and I didn't touch them. *You* lost them again."

"Dale, can you consider the possibility that you inadvertently put them somewhere?" I asked.

"Why on earth would I move your glasses?"

"That's exactly what I keep asking!" I replied.

Dale rolled her eyes. I feared she was slipping into a coma, but she actually became quite animated and energetic. "I'll look around the house," she said. "You go search the car."

I was tempted to ask her again about having a physical exam, but I decided not to risk it. Medical professionals will warn you that one does not want to tangle with an emotional woman who's suffering from projection and denial.

"They weren't in the car," I glumly reported a few minutes later.

"Did you look in the gap between your seat and the console? You're always losing things there—pens, notebooks, the checkbook," she said.

"I looked," I said.

"Did you look hard?"

---

for crying out loud, I'm not completely incompetent!

I snapped. "Yes, for crying out loud, I'm not completely incompetent! I looked and they aren't there."

The bottom line was that we didn't find either pair of glasses anywhere. So the next day I went to the One Hour Glasses place at the mall to order a new pair. I drove there in Dale's car because I had her tires rotated earlier that day. (Dale doesn't like to deal with mechanical stuff. I, on the other hand, have a great deal of "hands on" mechanical experience—defined as "handing money to a mechanic.")

I asked the glasses place people to give me the same prescription and lenses they had on file, but they no longer stocked the same frame. So I called Dale and asked her to meet me at the mall. (Even though I'm an adult male who's perfectly capable of making his own fashion decisions, Dale insists on going with me when I buy glasses, lest I come home with frames that she insists make me look like Harry Truman.)

Dale called me back within two minutes. "Let's play twenty questions," she said. "Guess what I found lodged into the space by the side of your car seat?"

I cringed. "A pack of gum?"

"Two pairs of glasses! TWO! I thought you looked there!" she said.

"But I did," I protested.

"Dave, my new motto is, 'If you can't find it, it must be there.'" She threatened to sew that little phrase into a cross-stitch, frame it, and hang it on the wall.

When I got home, she wasn't exasperated with me. She was laughing, and she gave me a big hug.

"You need me," she said. "You absolutely need me, or you would be doomed."

She was right. I was so appreciative I decided to take her out to dinner. I would have done the driving, but someone apparently moved my car keys.

When you stop and think about it, living with me day in and day out, putting up with all the little things I do that drive her up the wall, gives my wife many opportunities to exercise the spiritual gifts of patience, longsuffering, and mercy. So basically, my little idiosyncrasies constitute a ministry to her, providing abundant occasions to grow spiritually. I hope she's properly grateful for my part in this…not to mention my keen alertness in detecting psychological dysfunction.

9

Airport Insecurity and Other Fiascoes

To the trained eye of the airport security staff, everything about the traveler was suspicious.

For starters, he clearly had beads of sweat on his brow, though it wasn't hot outside and the airport terminal was cool. And he wore dark sunglasses even when inside the building.

As he checked in, the ticket agent noticed that the man had booked his arrival and return flights on different airlines, via far-flung cities that weren't remotely in line with his ultimate destination, and with absurdly long layovers. In short, he had an itinerary no rational traveler would choose. Furthermore, third-party payment was involved.

The alert agent therefore stamped his tickets with a bright red code to ensure he received extra scrutiny before he stepped foot aboard a plane.

The marked man was holding an overstuffed carry-on bag that he kept reaching into compulsively. When he got to the top of the escalator, he took one look at the passenger screening process, immediately took the downward bound escalator back to the lobby, and almost sprinted to the restroom.

When he finally returned to the screening area, the security agents were waiting for him.

"We'll need you to step over here for further screening," said the agent.

By "further screening" the agent meant, "By the time we're finished, you'll be able to tell your doctor he can skip the prostate exam this year."

While 99.9 percent of all passenger screenings are just an uneventful snoozer of a routine, this time you could tell all the red flags were up and the screeners were loaded for bear. If the guy so much as twitched a nostril, they'd have him handcuffed and spirited away to a secure facility before you could say "Gitmo."

"I want you to remove your belt, and then I'm going to use the back of my hand to pat down your sensitive area," said the security agent.

As a member of the concerned traveling public, I would have openly applauded the attentiveness and professionalism of the screeners on this occasion…were it not for the fact that *I* was the screenee.

Now, let me pause here and explain how I came to be involved in a situation where someone other than my doctor or my wife was taking an inordinate amount of interest in my susceptible sector.

Let's start with the beads of perspiration. Easily explainable. I was running late and missed the parking lot shuttle bus, so I'd trotted most of the way to the terminal. I'm not an athletic person. I'm a person who gets shortness of breath walking out to the mailbox in my front yard. Therefore, by the time I reached the ticket counter I was sweating like a prize fighter in the ninth round.

The reason I kept checking my bag while standing in line was simply the fact that I couldn't find my glasses. So I wore my sunglasses in order to actually see the gate numbers and not accidentally board a plane to Okinawa.

As to the suspicious itinerary, I was redeeming a "sorry we overbooked your flight, here's an apology" voucher that I received from an airline. This airline didn't have great connections to the city to which I was heading. Plus, when I booked the flight, they put me on a "sister airline" for my return, and that airline had even worse connections. My return trip would take me from Minneapolis to Chicago to Phoenix to Orlando to Australia to Saskatchewan to Sacramento. On the plus side, I got a slew of frequent flyer points.

And there's a perfectly innocent reason why I scampered down the escalator right after I ascended it. It had been a two-hour drive from my house to the airport, I'd been sipping coffee most of that time, and my bladder was stretched to the size of a life raft. My plan was to check in quickly so I wouldn't risk missing the final boarding call, but when I saw the long line of passengers moving at a sloth's pace through the screening process, I decided to run back down the stairs and unleash a mighty river of relief.

So although these actions seemed suspicious, I was utterly innocent of any vile intent.

"I want you to unbutton your pants," the screener said.

"Here? In front of everyone? Are you kidding?" I asked.

---

airport security people **do not** have a sense of **humor**

He was not kidding. Airport security people do not have a sense of humor. But they do have weapons. So I complied.

I fully expected him to say, "Now bend over and cough twice." But he gave my abdomen a cursory touch and decided I wasn't a threat after all, but merely a harmless idiot who needed to learn not to act like a potential hijacker, or else I just might find myself in an orange jumpsuit commencing an exciting career in the prison laundry business.

The truly awful thing about this fiasco was that it happened in front of scores of other passengers who then eyed me suspiciously throughout the flight. When I made my way down the aisle to use the lavatory, all eyes tracked me. No tennis ball at a Wimbledon match ever received more unison staring than I received in that airplane. Had I made any suspicious moves, such as yawning or blinking, I think my seatmate would have pummeled me to a pulp with his John Grisham novel.

It's hard to be misunderstood, but that's a part of life. It's definitely a part of marriage. Even when you mean well, even when your motives are pure, even when you can't begin to understand how you could be so terribly misunderstood—it's bound to happen.

One day when I was rather busy, I asked Dale if she could possibly run an important errand for me. She said she would.

As the day wore on, I realized she, too, had a lot on her plate, and I started to feel badly for asking her to take care of my errand. So I decided to take care of it myself, then pleasantly surprise her with the news that she need not worry about it.

After all, what better gift can you give a harried woman than the gift of free time? Besides, once I freed up some time for her, I figured she would be happy and grateful and the bonus time would allow us an opportunity to snuggle up on the couch in front of the fireplace and probably engage in a romantic interlude while the kids were out for the evening.

But when Dale found out I'd already taken care of the errand, her reaction was *not* "Oh, how sweet of you to be so considerate—let's make out!"

Rather, she was steamed.

"So," she huffed, "you figured you couldn't count on me."

"Not at all…" I began, stunned.

"Just because I didn't immediately pounce on it, you thought I would let you down. So you had to take care of it yourself."

"But I…"

"Or you think I'm too incompetent to run a simple errand. Is that it? I'm incompetent?"

"But Hon…"

"I'm so offended," she added.

"But actually I only wanted…"

"To make sure it got done," she snapped. "Well then, fine.

You can do *all* your errands yourself from now on. Since I'm sooooo much less efficient than you anyway…"

In case I didn't mention it, and in case you hadn't figured it out, this misunderstanding was significantly complicated by the fact that it just so happened to be that time of the month. As any professional firefighter will tell you, there's nothing quite so exciting as trying to put out a forest fire by dumping fifteen thousand gallons of gasoline on it.

By the time I was able to finally explain the situation to Dale, and fully articulate my pure-as-the-driven-snow motivation, she was no longer miffed and, in fact, liked me again.

"You're so sweet," she said, giving me a hug.

And though she subsequently directed me to remove my belt and gave me an extremely thorough frisking that far exceeded anything ever contemplated by the security people, I didn't complain. That's the kind of forgiving and spiritually mature husband I am. If that's the price for patching up a misunderstanding, I'm willing to pay it.

10

What's Cooking?

It was Dale's birthday, and I decided that instead of taking her out to dinner I would wait on her hand and foot at home. I would do all the cooking, including creating her favorite dessert—a strawberry shortcake. I would cover every tiny detail, right down to brewing her a perfect cup of English tea to accompany dessert. The entire menu would be a surprise.

"That's so sweet of you," she said, "but I don't mind helping."

"Nope, this is your special day and I'm going to handle it all. You just sit down and relax. Maybe read your favorite magazine."

She smiled and gave me a kiss.

"Thanks," she said.

I decided to make the shortcake first. Then it could be cool and ready to cut right after dinner. Efficiency and planning was the name of the game. I pulled the recipe card out of Dale's little box.

I realized I was in trouble when, instead of finding precise measurements, I saw ambiguous words like "a pinch" and "a dash." It also said I needed to "dust" flour on a "lightly greased" baking sheet. Trick words, all of them.

I was tempted to ask Dale for help, but I refrained. I mean, how hard could this be?

After five minutes of pawing through every nook and cranny of the kitchen, I finally called out, "Hon, where do we keep the grease?"

There was a long pause before she replied.

"Do you mean shortening or vegetable oil?"

I looked again at the recipe card. "It says 'grease.'" I said.

Pause.

"What are you making?" she asked.

"I can't tell you. But I need to grease a baking sheet."

"Then you need shortening," she said.

I frowned.

"Well, why didn't the card just say so?"

"Because it's a given," she said. "Everyone knows what it means."

Everyone but me, apparently.

I pressed on.

"Hon, you don't need to get up, but how much grease—I mean shortening—is meant by 'lightly,' and how much flour equals a 'dusting'?"

Pause.

"Dave, are you being serious?"

"Yes," I said.

"Can I come in the kitchen?"

"No. I'll bring the pan into you and you can look at it." I finished smearing the pan with a coat of white goo.

She glanced at it.

"That's much too thick. Just wipe it off with a paper towel and it will be fine. And then just sprinkle on just enough flour to stick. Make it look like the bookshelf you never used to dust when you were single."

Ahhh. Sensible instructions. Now we were getting somewhere.

"Dave, do you mind if I come in and make myself a cup of tea to have while I read my magazine?" Dale called from the living room.

"I'll get it, my sweet. You just stay put," I said.

I'd purchased a special imported tea, and I wanted it to be a surprise. I glanced at the box for the directions so I could steep the teabag the precise number of minutes.

"Dale, what exactly does it mean to 'bring to a furious boil'? And how would that differ from a 'full rolling boil,' which is what the next recipe calls for?"

There was a sigh from the other room.

"Both terms mean the same thing," she said.

These cooking people needed to get on the same page.

"Does a 'tsp.' mean a big spoon or a little spoon?" I asked.

"Little."

"And does it mean heaping, or flattened off?"

"Dave, can I come in and help? It would be, um, romantic to cook together," she said.

Hmmmm. That had possibilities.

"Well, you can come in and coach me," I said, "but you can't do any actual cooking."

At first she just issued tips and monitored my actions. But as things got hectic, I did allow her to grab a few ingredients and do a bit of stirring. Then I remembered I hadn't sliced up the vegetables, so I let her do some chopping while I went outside to fire up the grill and throw on a couple of steaks.

"How about if I just monitor things in here while you take care of the meat? We don't want it to burn," she said.

"Good thinking, my sweet. Keep an eye on the stove—just don't do any actual cooking. I want you completely relaxed."

"You got it," she said, throwing on an apron.

"Oh, and I forgot to set the table. Can you put the plates and silverware on the table?" I asked. "But do it in a relaxed fashion," I added, running outside to spray water on the bellowing conflagration.

When I brought the steaks inside, Dale was just finishing cutting up the last of the strawberries.

"Yikes," I said, "I guess I forgot that part."

"I was only slicing—which is different from cooking," she pointed out.

"You're right. This is all still according to plan."

The dinner was truly marvelous. Everything was cooked exactly right, the table looked great, and the shortcake was browned to perfection even though I don't quite recall actually kneading it or sticking it into the oven or ever checking it with a toothpick or removing it from the oven. I must have really been on a roll. When you get to be an accomplished chef, it all becomes second nature.

"It's absolutely wonderful," Dale said.

I beamed with pride. "And I did it all by myself," I said.

What's (Not) Cooking?

Because my wife has always been so spiritually stable, I was utterly shocked when she joined a bizarre cult. I had no clue anything was afoot until, at lunchtime one day, she tipped her hand.

"What's this?" I asked, staring at the weird food item she'd just set before me.

"It's a lettuce and tomato sandwich," she replied.

"Where's the bacon?" I asked.

"I thought we'd just skip the bacon this time," she replied.

"You can't have a BLT without the B!" I retorted, aghast.

"Dave, you don't have to have meat at every single meal."

So there it was. Raw heresy. Meatless meals? The very thought gave me the willies. Clearly, unless I could get her deprogrammed she would soon be dressed in a white tunic and selling small trinkets in the airport lobby.

"So you've decided to make us vegetarians. What false teacher has poisoned your mind?" I asked.

"Oh good grief!" she replied. "An *occasional* meal without meat doesn't make us vegetarians. You're so stuck in your ways. Just try something new for a change."

where would this madness end?

"What shall we change next?" I asked. "Shall we paint the White House orange? Or perhaps substitute a comic book for the church hymnal? Where will this madness end?"

She rolled her eyes.

To clear her mind, I knew I had to invoke brilliant, indisputable theology. "Dale," I said calmly, "if God never intended for us to eat bacon, how come it's made out of meat?"

I knew my brilliant stroke was a breakthrough, because she muttered, "Oh for heaven's sake!" and got out the frying pan.

But the theological battles are by no means over, because she just signed us both up to join an exercise cult. I tried to convince Dale that if God intended for us to jog, He would never have given us Lay-Zee-Sloth recliners.

But she's still in denial.

I can only hope for another breakthrough—and if I lie here long enough in the recliner, I know it will come.

The Many Merits of Marriage

Of the following two scenarios, which one sounds like more fun?

SCENARIO #1: You're a single guy sitting by yourself in a restaurant, and feeling alone. You poke your fork at your food and wish you'd ordered something else.

Finally, to break the boredom, you deftly switch plates with a diner nearby, and start enjoying his platter of barbecued ribs.

The outraged diner comes over and wrestles you for the plate, then phones the authorities. They book you in the county jail for misdemeanor possession of honey-glazed pork.

In the county jail, you're locked inside cramped quarters with another prisoner—also a single guy, and one who was arrested for misappropriating and ingesting someone else's bowl of chili. The hapless thief is moaning on his bunk and clutching his abdomen, which is the international signal for "I need some Tums." The shockwaves from your cellmate's lively abdominal detonations are bending the cell bars, and the accompanying fumes are literally peeling the paint off the wall.

SCENARIO #2: You're dining out with your spouse, and you each order different entrees so you can enjoy sharing each other's meal. After a lovely evening with no hint of police officers, mug shots, or Olympic-class flatulence, you head home to engage in a passionate evening of sweaty romance. Afterward, you drift off to sleep with the sweet knowledge that Congress recently increased the tax break for married couples.

Yes, marriage clearly has substantial benefits. But the advantages of matrimony don't stop at shared meals and tax breaks and delightful bouts of conjugal fellowship. There are uncounted oodles of advantages to marriage.

CAUTIONARY NOTE: I need to explain that when I use the term *marriage* I have in mind the traditional understanding of a heterosexual relationship that's commenced after you've repeated wedding vows in front of God and a minister and a bunch of friends and relatives and bridesmaids and groomsmen and a photographer and a cute little ring-bearer.

---

wish i didn't have to explain what marriage is, but i live in California

---

I wish I didn't have to explain what marriage is, but I live in California where the state legislature passed a bill defining marriage as "any consensual and sexual relationship between a man and a woman, or a man and a man, or a woman and a woman, or any combination thereof, including entire fraternities, or poodles, parrots, and other pets, or any small nocturnal rodents not protected under current state or federal endangered species statutes, and former President Clinton."

Okay, okay, they didn't go that far. But they did redefine marriage to include same-sex couples. And once you head down the slippery slope of defining marriage according to whatever sexual relationship someone wants to have, you've pretty much kissed off any meaning to the word marriage. And the implications for society are huge. (Governor Arnold Schwarzenegger vetoed the bill, but it was still a close call. The mere fact that our elected representatives passed a bill redefining marriage means that a majority of both houses in the legislature are in severe need of a brain enema.)

While I'm no marriage expert, I want to do my part in making the case for traditional marriage. My main credential is that I've been married to my beloved bride for nearly a quarter century. She's the only woman with whom I have, as the British writer Adrian Plass so discreetly put it, "disported in the altogether." And I'm the only man with whom she, as the French so eloquently express it, "made va-va voom!"

Which leads right into one of the big benefits of monogamous matrimony: We get to engage in utterly unprotected sex without the fear of communicating nasty sexually transmitted diseases that can eventually cause valuable parts of you to become covered in painful pustules and make it feel like you're emitting a stream of flaming Drano when you take a leak. And if I remain faithful to my wife I have no fear of contracting AIDS, which always results in a debilitating wasting away followed by certain death, which really cuts down on your love life. Capeesh?

Tune in next time when we explore just exactly what the Germans mean when they refer to "hankering for ein sauerkraut of desire."

13

The Hidden Benefits of Marriage

As noted in the previous chapter, a majority of the California Legislature is insane, and thus they passed a bill giving marriage all the sanctity of a public orgy during Gay Pride Month. And once a group of lawmakers abandons the legal concept of marriage as we've always known it, they've effectively opened Pandora's box.

And although the bill was vetoed, the main proponent of the "marriage-should-mean-whatever-anyone-wants-it-to-mean" movement has basically already warned Governor Arnold Schwarzenegger, "I'll be back!"

Why do I feel like I'm watching a scary science fiction movie?

Other writers have already outlined zillions of reasons why novel redefinitions of marriage are immoral and dangerous and idiotic, but I have my own list of additional reasons why traditional marriage is important.

Reason #1: Even though men realize it's in their best interest, and even though we're generally rational beings, no man would ever voluntarily get a prostate exam unless his wife made him do so. I am proof of this.

MY WIFE: "When is the last time you had a complete physical exam?"

ME: "Well, technically, at birth."

MY WIFE: "I'm making an appointment for you right now."

ME: "But I feel fine."

MY WIFE (dialing the doctor's phone number): "I'm making the appointment anyway, because I love you and I don't want to lose you to a preventable disease simply because you find the examination uncomfortable and somewhat embarrassing."

ME: "But my love, I'm quite confident that—"

MY WIFE (holding the phone): "Yes, Tuesday will be fine for his physical. And please ensure that he gets a prostate exam no matter how much he snivels and whines and claims there are grave national security implications."

If I asked another guy if he thought I needed a prostate exam, he'd say, "Nah. You've never had a problem there before, and you aren't dead yet, right?" Both of us would find this argument persuasive.

---

the sahara desert was once a fertile green land

Reason #2: Environmental scholars have long wondered why the Sahara Desert, which was once a fertile green land filled with the songs of colorful birds, became the gigantic blazing hot sand trap it is today. Well, recent research has revealed that a bunch of unmarried guys used to live there, hunkering down over primitive fire pits and watching primitive sit-coms on TV and never even thinking about dusting the furniture or cleaning under the bed, until eventually the entire ecosystem was overwhelmed by massive dust bunnies.

So when you turn on one of those nature shows on TV and

watch film clips of huge sand storms rolling across the dunes, think about what awaits YOUR part of the country if men stop marrying women.

Reason #3: There are lots of women who get mammograms only because they're pestered by their thoughtful and loving and insistent and unamused husbands (who just got back from their prostate exams).

HUSBAND: "Okay, I had my so-called 'digital exam' that had absolutely nothing to do with any form of mathematics I recall from high school. It's time for you to have a mammogram."

WIFE: "Oh good grief! You're simply retaliating because I made a doctor's appointment for you."

HUSBAND: "Not so, my love. The doctor reminded me that I need to keep after you because you need regular breast cancer screenings as a part of your routine health maintenance."

WIFE: "But the exam is so uncomfortable. You have no idea how it feels to…"

HUSBAND: "I'm making the appointment anyway, because I love you and I don't want to lose you to a preventable disease simply because you find the examination uncomfortable and somewhat embarrassing. Neener, neener, neener."

WIFE: "But I feel just fine and I have all these important things to—"

HUSBAND (Holding the phone and not hearing a word she's saying): "Yes, next Thursday would work fine for her. Yes, the new high-powered, high-resolution 'Clamps of Exceptionally Cold Glass' mammogram machine will be fine. Better safe than sorry. She's the love of my life, and I want to grow old with her."

That's the language of marriage.

The simple fact is that my marriage is demonstrably good for me. And it's good for my wife. Even if we ignored all the biblical arguments for marriage, or even gave the heave-ho to all the proven data about how kids do so much better if they grow up in a home with a mom and a dad who love each other, the research proves that married men and women who keep their vows are generally healthier, happier, and more satisfied with life than people who don't live life in a traditional marriage.

And now, when I'm watching sit-coms on TV, if my wife could just learn not to obstruct my view by dusting the furniture, and not to over-power the sound by running her vacuum cleaner. The dust bunnies can't be that bad—although, I'm not sure I would notice if they were.

"Two" Good to be True

Although the issue of human cloning poses serious ethical dilemmas, after considering both the pros and cons, I came down firmly in favor of cloning once I realized I could create an entirely new me to do all the yard work.

My wife, however, was somewhat less than enthusiastic about the idea.

"Have a glass of warm milk and a nap, and talk to me again once you're sane," Dale said.

Whereas I try to look on the bright side of technological innovations, my wife has serious skepticism issues.

"But my love," I told her, "think of all the possibilities of having two of me. I could be enjoying the comfort of my Lay-Zee-Sloth recliner and watching the World Series while the other me is outside trimming shrubbery and engaging in a host of other unpleasant tasks! It's the best of all possible worlds. The potential simply boggles the mind."

She folded her arms and frowned—which I'm learning, after twenty-five years of marriage, is *not* a sign of enthusiasm. "Peachy," Dale said. "Twice the number of ATM transactions that don't get recorded because 'someone' forgot. Twice the laundry. Twice the dirty dishes. And twice the belching. If you're just trying to double my irritation, you're succeeding," she added.

"Not to worry, my sweet," I replied. "The other me would technically still be me, but a much more disciplined version. I could require him to be helpful, to pick up his own socks without being asked, to walk the dog, and to perform oodles of other domestic chores. Since he wouldn't be the real me, he'd have no legal standing in our nation, and I could drop him little hints that he just might get deported unless he obeys my every whim." That's the kind of leverage I never in my wildest imagination dreamed of having, even with our kids.

Dale looked thoughtful.

"Let me ponder this for a moment," she said, tapping a finger to her temple. "I could replace you with another, more improved you. Yes, I'm beginning to see the plus side of the equation."

"Replace?" I asked. "Um, who said anything about replacing? This would be an additional me, not a replacement me!"

But she was staring off into space. "Wow. A you who would be helpful around the house. A you who would be out mowing the lawn and waxing my car and getting all tanned and physically fit. A cuter, kinder, more thoughtful you. It would be like turning back the clock to our newlywed days. I think this idea is growing on me. I might even want to go out to dinner with this you."

The hair rose on the back of my neck.

"You can't start dating the new me! It wouldn't even be me! You can't let that imposter ruin our marriage!" I yelped.

"Oh, I would never leave you," Dale said. "I wasn't kidding when I made my wedding vows. But the replacement you would still, technically, be you. You said so yourself. Same DNA, same fingerprints, same everything—but so much better than you. *He* could be the wedding vow version of 'for better,' while *you* could be the 'for worse.' And while *you're* watching boring television shows, he and I could be out on bike rides together. I guess we could consider letting you join us sometimes for a picnic at the park, as long as you brought your own lunch."

"You can't replace me with me! This is insane! I can't be the other man in our life!"

"But the technology's all there," Dale said.

"Well, it's wrong! It's unnatural! It's weird! You have to give up this madness," I pleaded.

"But I thought you *wanted* another you," Dale said.

"That was before I thought through the theological implications! I'm sure God had a very good reason for making only one of me!"

"Isn't that kind of rigid, old-fashioned thinking?" Dale asked.

I ran to our bedroom, threw on my work clothes, and bolted toward the garage. "I'm going to go mow our lawn," I told Dale on my way out. "If another me ever dares to even touch so much as a blade of my grass, I'll phone the authorities and have myself hauled off the premises for trespassing."

"Try to get a tan while you're out there," Dale called after me. "A tanned you is a more romantic you."

"You got it!" I replied. "And I'll get a good workout while washing and waxing your car! With enough time and exercise, I can look just as handsome as the fake me!"

"You're one of a kind," Dale said, blowing me a kiss.

"You know," I added, turning to Dale once more before tackling the lawn, "I don't think the world is ready for two of me."

"That makes two of us," Dale agreed.

An Unbearable Burden

My wife's purse is packed with so many pounds per square inch that I risked dislocating my shoulder one day when she asked me to carry it "for a few minutes" while she looked through racks of clothes at the mall.

In the witty manner that Dale finds so endearing, I asked her, "Hon, did you know your purse could double as a training device for those sturdy Eastern European female weight lifters?"

"Oh, I can lighten it easily," she replied. "All I have to do is take out your wallet, your keys, your pager, your phone, your breath mints, your lip balm, and your bottle of water, and I can drop two-thirds of the weight. Let's face it, Dave, it isn't my purse anymore. It's *our* purse."

I could literally feel my internal organs turn to Jell-O.

"That's not funny, Dale. You know how my back hurts if I drive with my wallet in my hip pocket."

"And your keys are too bulky, and so's your cell phone, and so's everything else. I don't mind that we have a joint purse," she added. "But *you* need to be willing to carry it, too."

"It isn't a joint purse!" I answered—in a whisper, lest any other shopper hear us.

But Dale wasn't listening. She found a dress she wanted to try on, and she asked me to stand by so I could tell her if it made her look pretty or awful (there's never a happy medium). But asking me to hold the purse while she tried on clothes indicated she didn't grasp the enormity of the crisis.

"Dale, I'll be standing in the women's clothing section holding a purse! People will think I'm cross-dressing!"

"Oh, stop overreacting," she said, blowing me a kiss as she walked to the dressing rooms.

She might just as well have dressed me up in a blonde wig and nylons. There was no way I was going to get caught like this. So I scampered over to the accessories section, hung her purse on a rack, and pretended to be shopping.

"Hmmm. I wonder what color purse I should buy for my wife, with whom I regularly engage in heterosexual activity," I said loudly, for the security cameras.

"Can I help you?" asked a fifty-something clerk.

"I am, uh, shopping for a gift for my wife," I said. "I would rather be watching football, on account of it's a very manly sport, but I'm taking time to find just the right something for her."

"Well, just let me know if I can be of any help," she said.

---

every muscle in my **body** was in rigor mortis **panic** mode

---

I was about to thank her when my phone began ringing. From the purse on the rack in front of me. I couldn't move. Every muscle in my body was in rigor mortis panic mode.

Ring.

"How odd," remarked the clerk, staring at the purses before us.

Ring.

I went into full projectile sweat mode as she pulled Dale's bag off the rack.

Final ring.

"Mercy, someone appears to have lost her purse," she remarked.

"How about those Rams?" I asked.

She opened the purse.

"Goodness, there's a man's wallet in here. Maybe we can contact the owner," she said flipping my wallet open.

She looked at the mug shot on the driver's license, then glanced up at me. Her hand fluttered to her mouth.

"I can explain everything," I said.

The phone rang again, and I grabbed it.

"Where are you?" Dale asked. "I thought you were going to wait for me outside the dressing room."

"Hon, this is an emergency. I'm going to hand the phone to this lady, and you need to tell her we're married, and I'm holding your purse because you made me, and this is all your fault."

Then Dale and the clerk had a riotously good chat, punctuated by much merriment and gasps for breath.

"You're soooooooo male," my wife said later when we were finally reunited.

I decided then and there to get a waist pack and carry all my own stuff. I figure I can even carry some of Dale's stuff when we go for walks or go camping.

And I'm reminded how, in a real way, our marriage helps us practice a biblical mandate: "Carry each other's burdens, and in this way you will fulfill the law of Christ" (Galatians 6:2).

I would feel even better about my new pack had Dale not pointed out that, realistically, it's nothing more than a purse you strap on your body.

I wonder if I can get her to wear it for me.

It's Not What I Prefer

I ripped open the envelope, glanced at the letter, and gasped.

I called to my wife. "Hon! We've been recognized as *Preferred Persons!*"

"Let me guess," Dale said. "We received yet another credit card offer from yet another Vice President of Marketing, who says our prudent financial history has earned us a new gold color on our current credit card. And you feel honored and impressed, because you never read the fine print—which, if you did, would reveal that anyone still paying bills on time and still breathing gets classified as 'preferred.' Dave, I threw away an identical offer just last week."

"Wrong, my beloved but cynical bride," I answered. "This is no credit card offer. This is bigger."

I held the slip of purple paper with the same awe and reverence I would afford the Hope Diamond.

I had recently given a speech to a college's alumni association, and while I knew my little chat had been appreciated, I never in my wildest dreams expected this. As a major sponsor of the annual aircraft show in my hometown, the college had just furnished me with a "Preferred Parking" permit to the popular event.

i performed the preferential parking dance of festive joy

I could scarcely contain my glee as I waved the paper at Dale. "Hon, we've been bestowed with the incredible honor of preferential parking! Do you have any idea what this means?" I asked, as I performed the preferential parking dance of festive joy.

"It means," Dale said, "that we'll be at the back of the line when we leave. The traffic will be awful. I don't think this parking pass is such a big deal."

I gasped. "It isn't just about proximity to the flight line," I explained. "It's about being classified as *Preferred!* We're part of the elite! We get to park in the exclusive area reserved for those who have been deemed worthy. It's a high honor, like having the Queen of England grant you a knighthood amidst the blare of regal trumpets and a lavish feast of kidney pie and boiled shrubbery!"

"You need a nap," Dale said.

Sadly, no matter how many times I explained the incredible honor symbolized by the PP emblem stamped on the pass, my wife couldn't grasp the enormity of the tribute we'd received. Every time I began to wax poetic about the staggering implications of our new status as persons of preference, she folded her arms and said, "It's *only* about parking in a baking hot lot at the airport. You have *not* been handed the keys to Buckingham Palace."

Sigh. It was no use. Giving my wife a Preferred Parking Pass was akin to handing an iPod to a bewildered indigenous person from the Amazon jungle, who then proceeds to use it as an implement to scrape fish scales off the daily catch. No clue.

The day finally came for the air show. Knowing that the mark of a truly sophisticated man is the ability to be restrained and cool while basking in the privileged life, I drove up to the parking attendant and casually mentioned, "We have a Preferred Parking Pass, as you can see by this purple document engraved with the coveted PP emblem."

"Yeah," he groused, "you and everyone else who paid the extra two bucks. Pull into that field over there with the rest of the mob."

Oh.

"PP stands for 'pathetic person,'" Dale whispered.

"For by the grace given to me I say to everyone among you not to think of himself more highly than he ought to think" (Romans 12:3 ESV).

17

Leading by Decree

After listening to a particularly inspiring sermon about "servant-leadership," I decided to emit more leadership in my marriage. On the drive home that Sunday, I issued my first leadership directive to my wife.

"Hon, the man has determined that he'll henceforth issue authoritative decrees in order to obtain the results he wishes."

Dale slowly turned to stare at me. *"The man?* Since when do you refer to yourself in the third person? And what in the world do you mean by issuing 'decrees'?"

"I'm just implementing today's sermon about leadership," I replied.

Dale's eyes narrowed. "Dave, did you hear *anything at all* the pastor said?"

---

clearly, I needed to take **charge**

I could sense that my initial attempt at imposing servant-leadership was not being well received. Clearly, I needed to "take charge."

"The man," I went on, "has issued a manly pronouncement, and will not change his mind. I've decreed that I shall take you out to lunch today. Then, the man decrees that he shall do a bunch of additional domestic duties this week so his spouse may finish that watercolor painting she has been putting off but really wants to finish. The man will accept no dissent."

"Dave, I think you've lost a few—"

I interrupted, waving my hand in an imperial, leadershipish manner. "The man has *more* decrees," I said. "The man also decrees that he and the wife of his youth shall take that vacation to Canada which she has always dreamed of, and have high tea at that hoity-toity place she's always wanted to visit. Thus it has been decreed, and thus it shall be done."

"Dave, I have a few decrees of my own. First, I decree that you're a lunatic and I love you. Second, I decree that you can keep up these servant-leader actions, but you can knock off the royal pronouncements. Third, I decree that if you follow my decrees, we'll be a very happy couple."

The man decreed that he agreed. And the couple is very happy indeed.

PART 2

Don't Try This at Home
A Man and His Kids

18

The Five-Phase Survival Guide
to Parenthood

The *first* thing any expecting mom needs to understand is that even if she does absolutely everything right—eats plenty of green vegetables, visits her doctor regularly, takes special vitamins during pregnancy—her adorable infant can nevertheless eventually mutate into an irrational, demanding creature that pediatricians refer to as a "teenager."

When you and your spouse decided to enjoy a romantic (albeit sweaty) little interlude resulting in a pregnancy, I bet you didn't pause to consider whether you could afford a huge future investment in basketball shoes.

No, you two besotted lovers were simply enjoying the bliss of the moment. That's because God, in his wisdom, designed sex to temporarily reduce your IQ to the level of broccoli. If we were utterly rational, we would be terrified to bring potential teenagers into the world. So God made sex such a powerful force that we forget, for a few brief moments, just what a pain we were to live with when *we* were teens. And thus God continues to propagate the human race.

If you feel like you've been manipulated by God—well, you have. He will, in fact, have His way. He likes to create new people. And if He has to reduce you to a brainless, helplessly compliant participant in His divine plan, He'll do precisely that. But you can hardly complain. You enjoyed every minute of it.

The following short but nevertheless informative survival

guide is intended to help you navigate the next several years of parenting.

PHASE ONE: You will notice, right off the bat, that your baby has serious deficiencies when it comes to personal hygiene. Your baby will therefore need your extremely personal service several times per day.

Because God is all powerful, He could have made your infant self-cleaning. But He didn't. Changing the baby is therefore clearly not simply about changing the baby. It's about changing *you*. God is deliberately putting you in a position where you have to make hard sacrifices for the sake of love.

Get used to it. Sacrifice is inherent in parenting. And if you see parenting as part of God's ongoing effort to mold you into the image of Christ, it will really enhance your view of parenting.

PHASE TWO: When our first baby, Mark, entered the phase of life commonly known as "the terrible twos," he would often ask to go to his favorite store.

"I want to go to Toys 'R Mine!" he would beg.

Don't believe any parenting book that says children are a blank slate and simply respond to their environment. They look sweet and innocent, but the default setting of the nature they bring into this world is far different. It's set on being selfish, pugnacious, and vehemently opposed to eating strained peas or anything else that's remotely good for them. It's your job to shape and mold them away from this default position.

---

it's **wise** to keep two-year-olds from acquiring **weapons**

You're going to be amazed at just how angry, flipped out, and livid a two-year-old can be. It's therefore wise to keep them from acquiring weapons, especially if you're making them take a nap when they would prefer to be smearing Jell-O on the walls.

As you see just how awful and selfish a toddler can be, you'll feel a powerful motivation to help them grow up to be better than that. Bear in mind that God has this same impulse when He thinks about you. He isn't content to leave you as you are. So God is molding and shaping you, just as you mold and shape your child. That's why divine discipline is a part of your life. You may not like it at the time, but it's for your own good.

PHASE THREE: Typically, there's a fairly long phase, lasting until about fifth or sixth grade, when your kids really look up to you, want to be with you, and are delighted to do things with you. Enjoy every second of this phase.

This is also when you children are most teachable. Have those family devotions and read to them from Bible storybooks.

Relish these years, because the split second the teenage hormones kick in, your kid will be horrified to discover you're extremely uncool, and he'll ask you to drop him off two blocks from school lest any of his friends think you and he are somehow related. Your teen may even deny he has parents. He may tell people he was formed in a petri dish as part of a secret government experiment. That's how embarrassing you've become.

The main lesson you'll learn in this phase is humility.

PHASE FOUR: The next phase is marked by raging hormones, wild mood swings, and irrational conversations. Yes, it's that time of the month for mom. Unfortunately, it's also that time of the *year* for your teenagers.

Just try to endure it, and get them plugged into a really good church youth group. While you want to be available to your teens, they also need the input of other significant adults.

I think a good youth pastor is worth his weight in diamonds. Make sure he gets steady raises. He deserves them.

PHASE FIVE: Your kids finally reach the age when it's time to let them go. There have been many wonderful memories, and also times of darkness and perhaps even despair. You would give anything to spin back the clock and wrestle on the floor with your eight-year-old kid, or teach your daughter again how to bake cookies, but you can't.

What you can do, and what you must do, is commend them to the grace of God and pray for them. And even though your parenting role is officially over, you'll always be mom or dad, always love them, and always be gladly willing to lay down your life for theirs.

And you understand the heart of God in a whole new way.

19
The Games People Play

The woman was simply in the wrong place at the wrong time. There was really no other reasonable explanation for the resulting catastrophe. Nevertheless, *I* got the blame.

This is not a just world.

My childhood home was located next to a busy street, and

cars cruised by all day at thirty-five miles per hour. At least, that was the posted speed limit. Many cars went faster. Tragically, the aforementioned lady was a speeder. All my rudimentary calculations had been based on the assumption that cars would be obeying the law, and had this lady been a decent law-abiding citizen, catastrophe would have been avoided.

I tried to make this point to my parents later on, but they were clearly looking for a scapegoat.

As I said, this is not a just world.

It was a warm June day, and one of my younger brothers and I had been playing with the hose in the front yard. Spraying each other got old pretty quickly, but because we were analytical and bright young boys we quickly turned our attention to the interesting world of science.

And what better science experiment can there be than calculating the precise moment at which one would need to fire a burst of water into the street in order for the aforementioned water to hit the windshield of an oncoming automobile that's traveling at exactly thirty-five miles per hour?

In a scientific manner, we developed a testable hypothesis about where we would have to place the nozzle in ratio to the path of the oncoming traffic. My dad's car was parked at the curb in front of our house, and it proved to provide an ideal base from which to conduct our research. By having me crouch near the front bumper, we could conceal the apparatus from the approaching control subject. The element of surprise was crucial to our study, as there was a high probability the control subject would alter its speed or trajectory if our intentions were known. Technically, scientists are supposed to get a written authorization from a test subject, but we were only eight and six years old, respectively, and therefore unaware of standard proto-col (not that this defense was even remotely persuasive to our parents).

We divided up the implementation duties, with me operating the water propulsion device while my brother hid in the tree and called out the countdown to T minus Zero.

Our first attempt was a failure. My brother miscalculated the correct time to call out his command to fire, and I reacted too late. The water splashed uselessly behind a 1965 blue Ford sedan.

We practiced test-firing between actual cars, and quickly recalibrated our command-and-control sequence to perfect the delivery system.

If the next car was cruising by at thirty-five miles per hour, our calculations showed that the unsuspecting driver would receive a surprising but nevertheless harmless splash of H_2O right smack in the middle of the windshield. We hadn't yet determined any practical use for our research, but sometimes you just do science for the sake of science and trust that future generations will benefit. My brother and I were magnanimous in that way, selflessly blazing the way for future researchers.

it's **hard** to feel too terribly **bad** for what happened next

Regrettably, our control subject chose to arrogantly violate the duly posted speed limit. So, really, it's hard to feel too terribly bad for what transpired next. She had to be doing at *least* thirty-seven miles per hour. Plus, she had unwisely left her front passenger side window rolled down. I certainly cannot be blamed for her negligence. I ask you, if *you* were driving home from Estelle's Beauty Parlor, where you'd just forked over twelve dollars to have your hair formed into one of those massive "bee hive" hairdos so popular when Lyndon Baines Johnson was President, wouldn't you have rolled up your window on the chance that an errant blast of water—perhaps from a faulty fire hydrant—might come flying into your car?

Soldiers report that sometimes, in the heat of battle, time seems to slow to a crawl and they can absorb in minute detail everything going on around them. Such was my experience at T minus Zero.

She may have been doing thirty-seven, but her car seemed to crawl by as the stream of water shot forcefully from the nozzle. Not a single drop besmirched her windshield as she sailed by me at those critical two extra miles per hour. The entire bolt of liquid blasted right into the hair hive, virtually obliterating two hours of Estelle's most recent professional effort.

I watched, as if viewing a slow motion film, as her eyes bulged forth in shock and dismay. Her hands flew momentarily off the steering wheel and clutched her soggy scalp as a shriek of distress and woe punctured what had been an otherwise sleepy summer afternoon.

Time snapped back to normal as she hit the brakes and skidded to a stop.

I dropped the hose and bolted into the house and was already hiding under my bed when a rather furious pounding commenced at our front door.

I shall spare you the traumatic aftermath of our research project gone awry. Suffice it to say our superiors stepped in and halted all further project development. They also halted my ability to sit down for the next three weeks.

My youth was filled with equally stupid antics. I think boys have a genetic disposition to recklessness and risk, and even though boys eventually transform into ostensibly mature and responsible men, we never completely escape that inherited predisposition (which helps explain the game of hockey).

So it shouldn't have shocked me when my own two boys began engaging in adventurous (read: hazardous) and novel (read: stupid) forms of play. But they took it to an entirely new level.

When the boys were in first and third grades, we lived on a corner lot where the entire front lawn was bordered by a tall L-shaped hedge that stopped at the driveway. We had cautioned the boys that because of the hedge it would be almost impossible for drivers to see them if they suddenly darted into the street from our driveway. They didn't interpret this as a warning so much as a dare.

They also invented an adventurous and novel (see the earlier definitions) new game called "dodge car." The rules were quite simple. Boy A sat in a little red wagon and steered it with the handle bent backward while Boy B pushed from the rear. As a car rounded the blind corner, the wagon was shoved from behind the hedge right into the path of the oncoming vehicle long enough to cause the driver to scream in panic while suffering an involuntary hygienic faux pas, but not long enough to result in actual contact with the front bumper. At the last possible moment, Boy B would yank the wagon back into the safe zone, and Boy A would then get out and do the pushing for the next round.

Play would continue until a shaken and incoherent driver staggered to our front door and explained how he had just nearly run over our child. And then asked to use our bathroom.

I did the standard apoplectic parent tirade and ended that particular little game. But, boys being boys, they found plenty of other insane tricks in the coming months and years. I attribute their current ability to breathe to the unflagging attention of guardian angels.

Generally speaking, impulsiveness is a bad thing. Something comes to mind, and if it sounds like fun, we don't stop to think it through.

You'd think we'd learn. But humans have an impulse to behave, well, impulsively. We spend years learning from our impulsive mistakes and finally, wisely, develop the habits of self-discipline and restraint. Or, if we don't, we end up making bad decisions, buying cars we can't afford, getting into dumb relationships, getting hooked on bad habits, or even getting impeached.

The seventh chapter of Proverbs is devoted to the issue of impulsive sexual activity. In it, a young man is propositioned by a prostitute. He listens to the pitch, then makes an impulsive choice:

> All at once he followed her like an ox going to the
> slaughter, like a deer stepping into a noose, till an
> arrow pierces his liver, like a bird darting into a snare,
> little knowing it will cost him his life.
>
> PROVERBS 7:22–23

Impulsive, rash, thoughtless actions have resulted in so much heartache and loss over human history. How many sexually transmitted diseases could have been avoided? How many AIDS deaths? How many divorces, how many destroyed relationships, splintered families? How many tragedies would not have unfolded?

While the Bible urges us to resist these impulses, there's one impulse that the apostle Paul urges us to obey—the impulse to bolt from temptation. "Flee the evil desires of youth, and pursue righteousness, faith, love and peace with those who call on the Lord out of a pure heart" (2 Timothy 2:22). We can train ourselves to flee the wrong impulses and obey the noble ones.

Soldiers learn to stay and fight for their unit when the natural impulse is to run away. Secret Service agents train themselves to literally step into the line of fire to protect the President from harm. These are selfless, heroic impulses. But they're built upon the foundation of self-discipline and training.

As parents, our calling is to train our kids out of their bad impulses. To teach them delayed gratification, and to take the long view.

But first, we must train ourselves. Because our kids are walking, breathing hypocrisy detectors, and they learn 90 percent of their values by watching us, not listening to us.

That's no mere hypothesis. It's a time-tested fact.

The Race Is On!

The great lumbering giant flailed his arms and roared as he lurched through the playground in pursuit of the shrieking children.

Kids scattered everywhere—climbing up the slides, shimmying up poles, scampering to the top of the jungle gym.

My two boys, Mark and Brad, loved it when I chased them at the local park. They also feared it. I think they loved it because they feared it. They loved the adrenaline rush when, standing safely at a distance and poised to bolt, they called out, "Come and get me, big dumb monster!"

Properly outraged at this taunt, the creature would set down his cup of McDonald's coffee, then rise in fury. The chase was on. I was no longer Dad; I was a mutant Goliath, a horrible ogre, a beast from the forbidden forest.

It took approximately twelve seconds before every other kid at the park was calling out, "Can I play too?" or "Catch *me*, ugly giant!"

The kids were fast, but I was faster. And I would make unexpected moves, suddenly rushing up the slide and grabbing Mark's leg or dashing to the jungle gym before the gaggle of kids could climb down.

Their eyes would bug out like ping-pong balls when they realized the monster had them trapped. Fortunately, the kids learned that the monster was basically an idiot who could be easily distracted if the prey simply pointed behind him and said, "Look, a comet!"

The monster fell for it every time, letting go of the clever kid and allowing a fast escape.

But the day finally came when the monster couldn't catch the kids, even while really trying. The monster was getting shortness of breath and kept asking for time outs, and the kids were getting faster by the day.

As more time passed, the kids no longer wanted to be chased.

And then they outgrew the playground.

So chase them while you can, dad. Make a fool of yourself in public. Win those sprinting contests while you still have the advantage! Enjoy every second of it, because it ends all too soon.

For an adult, a span of ten years isn't all that dramatic. Sure, I'm balder and heavier at forty-seven than I was at thirty-seven, but I'm not a radically different person. But the younger you are, the more difference a decade makes. The difference between an eight-year-old and an eighteen-year-old is the difference between a third grade kid playing soldier during recess and a U.S. Marine fighting terrorists in Afghanistan.

I used to wrestle with my boys when they were little. I began hesitating when they started winning a few. And I flat quit when it began to hurt.

But one day a strategic and exceptionally rare opportunity opened up when my son Brad was seventeen. I'd been working out, I was feeling pretty good, and given the particular circumstances of the moment, I had a high degree of confidence that I could beat him in a sprint. I was so confident that I raised the stakes.

"Want to race?" I asked him.

He rolled his eyes.

---

i **bet** him five hundred dollars I could race and **beat** him

---

I pointed into the distance. "I'll bet you five hundred dollars I can beat you to *there,*" I said. Normally I'm not a gambling man. But like I said, this was a rare and special case.

"Five hundred bucks? Are you serious?"

I positioned my right foot at an imaginary starting line. "Ready, set, GO!" I said.

And off we went, shuffling slowly down the hospital corridor as Brad gripped the mobile stand that held the intravenous fluid bags and tubes feeding medications and antibiotics into his body.

It had been a hard couple of weeks for my son. His abscessing appendix had been poisoning him for days before the condition was finally diagnosed. He was admitted to the hospital two days before Christmas, endured emergency surgery, spent several days in the intensive care ward, and was now in his second week of slow and painful recovery.

He was utterly fatigued, but the doctors told him he had to get up several times each day and walk. He needed movement. He needed exercise if he was going to recover. But he was starting to balk at the medical directives. He hurt, he was tired, and he was depressed after learning he had to spend at least another week in the hospital because his white blood cell count was still way out of whack.

I figured a race for prize money would help motivate him. And it did. It took him ten minutes to get within striking distance of the finish line, but I would say he easily cut two minutes off his previous personal best time.

But even with his improved effort I was still leading, and I was barely winded. I could almost taste the victory and hear the roar of the crowd.

"First one to touch the wall wins!" I said to Brad as we sprinted in an extremely leisurely fashion toward the goal.

"You have to at least give me a chance," he replied, imperceptibly picking up the pace.

The wall loomed before us. The race was neck and neck. The competitors both reached out, their fingers just inches from the goal.

I leaned forward and touched the wall.

"I WON!" I shouted, doing the happy dad victory dance.

Brad looked at me, stunned.

"Admit it," I said. "I'm in better shape than you!"

"You're so lame," he answered.

"Listen up," I told him. "You need to get healthy more than you need to get loot. And you need to walk this hall a lot. You have to do it even though it hurts. But here's the deal: If you'll get out of this place, if you'll get healthy, if you get to the point where you're in good enough shape to scuba dive again—I'll take you someplace special."

"Where?" he said, eyes brightening.

"You'll find out when you check out of the hospital. And the prize is worth way more than five hundred bucks," I said.

We couldn't easily afford it, but Dale and I had agreed to take a family vacation to Maui when Brad was in good enough shape. We'd wanted to go for years. We needed to just *do* it, or it wouldn't happen. After all Brad had been through, we wanted to do this for him—and for all of us.

But we kept it a secret from Brad. I think it was good lung exercise for him to keep asking, "Where? Why can't you just tell me now?"

So he walked. He got stronger every day. After his third week in the hospital, he was finally ready to be released, though he was still in the early stages of getting back to his full strength.

His recovery continued at home, aided by the attention of his devoted mom and many friends who checked in on him regularly.

the day **finally** came when I needed to make **good** on the bargain

The day finally came when I needed to make good on my end of the bargain.

"Brad, we're going to go someplace tropical," I said.

"Where?"

"It starts with an M and ends with a…"

"What?" he pleaded.

I pretended I suddenly hurt my finger.

"Owie!" I said, shaking my hand.

"Mexico?" Brad asked.

"What?" I replied.

"You said it started with an M. But what did you do to your hand?" he asked.

"We're going to Maui, Brad! Get it? 'M' and 'owie' equals Maui!" I said.

He couldn't have been more excited.

We booked the trip several months later to ensure that Brad was fully recovered and ready to dive. When we finally got to the island, Brad had the privilege of diving in one of the most extraordinary places of God's creation.

It was a big bright spot in his life after what had been a truly terrible ordeal. He'll never forget it. And I'll always remind him that, as awful as the entire hospital experience was, and as much as he would like to forget it, the fact still remains that *I won the race.*

Hey, when you get my age, you have to snatch every victory you can.

21

Death by Purple

I'm both proud and impressed by the professionalism and courage displayed by our troops in Iraq and Afghanistan, yet I must admit I was shocked and even horrified when I heard a disturbing foreign news service report about some of the "tactics" being used by our soldiers.

This report included an alarming assertion (which you'll wish to keep away from small children and the squeamish). It said that when prisoners refused to cooperate during interrogation, they were exposed for prolonged periods of time to music from children's TV programs, such as *Barney*, to make them more willing to talk. Furthermore, the report stated, such tactics were labeled by Amnesty International as possibly constituting torture.

Listen, I love our troops. I support them a hundred percent, I pray for them, and I've even sent packages of Christmas gifts to soldiers I don't even know as part of an Adopt-a-Soldier program. I have friends in the armed forces. But if I was called as an expert witness in a military trial, I would have to agree that sustained exposure to the Barney theme song is not only torture, but it may qualify as a Weapon of Mass Destruction.

I'm no armchair critic. As a survivor of excessive, forced exposure to children's music, I've personally experienced the trauma, the night sweats, the horror, the shivers, and the abject longing for the sweet release of death.

When my children were of preschool age, they were given musical tapes as birthday gifts. These gifts were given by people who were cleverly camouflaged as my kids' friends, but who, in retrospect, were clearly tiny enemy agents.

The song our boys loved most droned on and on about bus wheels going around and around and around, all through town. A so-called "musician" sang these *same words* over and over and over for nearly six hours, until he reached a final rousing chorus that was only more of the same, except it ended with this line: "until your daddy finally snaps and jumps in front of the bus!"

i'm no armchair critic

When the song was mercifully over, the kids would say, "Play it again, Daddy!" so we could all hear it again. If this kind of abuse isn't forbidden by the Geneva Convention, it should be.

Here's the conundrum—there's some really high quality children's programming out there. *Sesame Street,* for example, does in fact both inform and entertain young children. It teaches good lessons about sharing and forgiving and being kind. It teaches the alphabet and counting games. There are also high quality programs put out by various Christian organizations. Focus on the Family has produced some great materials that teach moral lessons and biblical truth. A quality video or DVD can be also be a great way to briefly occupy your five-year-old while you and your wife sneak into the bedroom for a quick episode of conjugal romper-room.

We're grateful we had this material available to us when our kids were little. The music could get kind of old, but it was usually pretty clever.

But unlike *Sesame Street* and the *Adventures in Odyssey* programs, *Barney* has no redeeming qualities at all. Small children nevertheless love him. Barney is the TV equivalent of a demon from hell, appearing as an angel of Purple. All parents, every last one of them, detest Barney. Even nice Christian people who dislike no one else are united in their visceral loathing of the Purple Spawn of Hades. If you do a Google search of the term "I hate Barney," you'll come up with 2,360 hits. You'll find "I Hate Barney" theme songs, chat rooms, blogs, and general grousings. Some of these sites and postings are quite violent and nasty. I'm not excusing this, but I do understand it.

So yes, prolonged exposure to this stuff is torture. I have no doubt that even the most hardened insurgent will eventually crack after a thousand choruses of the Barney theme song.

I hate to admit that, deep down, I take glee in the knowledge that hundreds of nineteen-year-old soldiers—young men who, not so many years ago, made their parents play the Barney tape over and over and over—had to drive around in Humvees that blared profoundly irritating music from enormous speakers which press reports describe as being "big as footlockers."

God is not only giving these young men the opportunity to serve their country. He's preparing them for fatherhood.

Play it again, soldier. And if you ever get hauled into court by Amnesty International, I will testify that, since you also had to listen to the Barney song, you've already been punished enough.

22
Dropping the Ball

All in all, I'd have to say he was one of the worst jugglers I've ever seen. When Mark and Brad were small, my wife and I were out for a stroll with them, and we happened upon a street performer who entertained for whatever loose change the crowd was willing to toss into his hat.

We quickly understood why he was a street performer as opposed to a member of the American Jugglers Association (if there is such a thing.) He kept dropping the balls. I mean, *all the time*. He would do okay for maybe thirty seconds, and the gaggle of kids were wide-eyed in amazement. But he didn't just drop the balls one or twice. It was basically raining balls. Stevie Wonder could have juggled almost as well as this guy.

The kids began to giggle, and the adults started to move on. But then the would-be juggler called out, "If you think *that* was terrible, watch this!"

He pulled four bowling pins out of his bag. The kids were again riveted, and pulled their parents back into the circle of spectators.

"I was pretty bad, wasn't I?" the juggler asked one little boy.

"Uh huh," replied the kid.

"But do you want to see what I can do with bowling pins?" he asked.

"Yes!" shouted the kids.

He began with two.

"Kids, it isn't easy to juggle," he said as he tossed the spinning pins into the air again and again. "I'm pretty good with just two pins. I could probably keep doing two of them for a long time and never drop one, but that would be boring. So should I risk adding a third one?"

"Yes!" the kids called back.

"Okay, here goes. Now this is harder," he said, throwing a third pin into the mix. "But four pins will be a lot harder. Should I try four?"

"YES!" shouted the kids.

"Okay!" he replied, and then there were four pins flipping and spinning—until they began falling and bouncing on the ground.

"I could just quit, but I don't believe in quitting," he said, gathering the four pins and tossing them back into the air. "If we just quit when things are hard, how will we ever get better? I get embarrassed when I drop things, and I'm not as good as a lot of jugglers, but if I keep working at it, do you think I can maybe get better?" he asked.

"YES!" the kids shouted.

"I think you kids could learn to juggle, too," he said, keeping his eyes on the spinning pins. "But you may want to try something else. Maybe you want to play baseball or basketball, or maybe you want do ballet. I guarantee you'll make mistakes, and drop the ball, and mess up. And you'll feel embarrassed and want to quit. But if you keep at it, you'll just get better and better."

He fumbled and dropped the pins.

"Kids, I'm not very good, am I? Should I just quit now?"

"NO!" yelled the kids.

"Well, I was thinking of maybe trying to juggle a ball, an apple, a bowling pin, and a bowling ball all at once. But that would be really hard, and I might fail. Should I just give up?" he asked.

"NO!" the kids thundered.

And he did it. He juggled all four of those objects. For fifteen seconds.

The crowd went wild. Parents stuffed bills into his hat. And Brad and Mark walked away with a great lesson.

All in all, I'd have to say he was one of the best jugglers I've ever seen.

23

Come Out of the Darkness

In a restaurant one day, our son Brad jogged back from the men's room, dove into the booth, and slid down in his seat until his eyes were level with his plate.

"There's a mad guy in the bathroom," he whispered.

Just then a man emerged from the men's room. Brad slouched his ten-year-old body further down into his seat. The man cast a glare around the dining room, then headed back to his seat in another section of the restaurant.

"Did something happen?" I asked Brad.

"Well, you're the one who always gives us those lectures about money not growing on trees. So it was a habit," he replied.

"You didn't…" I began.

"I turned the light off when I was leaving," he replied.

"Did you turn it back on?"

Brad shook his head.

---

it **scared** him so much he just **ran** for it.

"He started yelling and stuff, and it scared me so much I just ran for it. But then I realized why he was yelling, so I turned back around and reached in and turned it back on. But he was, like, using all these bad words and stuff and so it was kind of like it served him right. So I turned it back off."

I'm not quite sure Brad's actions passed the "What Would Jesus Do" test. But because I try to find the bright spot (so to speak) in these kinds of episodes, I do find two biblical lessons to apply.

First, just as Jesus taught, we need to walk in the light or we will stumble in the darkness:

> Then Jesus told them, "…Walk while you have the light, lest darkness overtake you. The one who walks in the darkness does not know where he is going. While you have the light, believe in the light, that you may become sons of light." When he had finished speaking, Jesus left and hid himself from them. (John 12:35–36 ESV).

Second, according to this passage, sometimes after you teach someone a good moral lesson, it's okay to hide.

24
Road Trip

My parents are of sturdy Midwestern stock, and they have that "let's just make the best of it" philosophy that's so common among those hardy souls who lived through the Great Depression and learned to make their own clothes from scrap iron. But even by the stoic standards of South Dakota, my mom and dad took "making the best of it" to novel heights.

Early in their marriage, they decided to bid good-bye to their native South Dakota (with its associated blizzards) and move to sunny California (with its associated earthquakes). As the flock of little Meurer kids steadily increased, topping out at five of us, Mom and Dad decided we needed to return for a visit to the relatives back east lest we children be deprived of the opportunity to meet scores of cousins and to view endless quadrants of flat and boring land.

The key challenge was transportation. We were a family of modest means, so getting seven of us back to South Dakota was a stretch. All the available options had drawbacks.

Flying was the easiest and most efficient choice, but the cost would have equaled the gross domestic product of Jamaica. So that was out.

The bus was more affordable. But we had a limited amount of vacation days, and with all the stops and vehicle changes that bus travel required, we would have had just enough time to disembark, shake hands with our cousins, and reboard for the trip home.

Driving a large family station wagon would have been a reasonable option were it not for the fact that we didn't own a large family station wagon. We owned a gas-sucking Chevy sedan and a gas-sipping 1963 Volkswagen Bug. Obviously, cramming seven people into the Bug for a roundtrip journey of 3,800 miles was logistically unfeasible and clearly absurd.

So we did it anyway. What a native Midwesterner calls "making the best of it," the rest of the planet dubs "madness of the highest order."

A vintage VW Bug contains a cubby hole behind the back seat, which is where the youngest tot rode. Three more children sat in a back seat designed for two, but we were young and small, and after Mom applied the grease and the shoe horn, we fit just fine.

That left only one more child, and this one was placed in the third front seat.

Now, Volkswagen enthusiasts will point out that there was no such thing as a third front seat in a 1963 Bug. Well, there was in ours. Dad built a tiny seat on top of the emergency brake. It made shifting a bit tricky, and the emergency brake was rendered inaccessible and therefore utterly useless in the event of an actual brake-related emergency, but the configuration allowed for all seven of us to actually fit inside the car and hit the road.

My parents had wisely stocked the car with Etch-a-Sketches, drawing pads, coloring books, and various other distracting items that did a marvelous job of occupying our attention for the better part of ten minutes. Then the troops began to get restless.

"He's breathing my air," I said, elbowing my younger brother.

"So hold your breath," Dad said.

"Make her stop looking at me."

"Close your eyes and you won't see her," Dad replied.

"I need to go to the bathroom."

Dad was clearly unamused and in no mood to stop. But

hey, if Mom needed to go, she needed to go. If it was simply us kids complaining, Dad would make us "hold it" until our bladders were the size of watermelons.

So we pulled into a gas station where we all spilled out. The attendant approached the car and blinked, and you could watch him counting and recounting us.

"Seven people in a *Bug?*" he asked my dad.

"Yep. Great gas mileage."

"Where you heading?" the attendant asked, as he cleaned the windshield.

"Sioux Falls," Dad said. "South Dakota."

"All the way to South Dakota, seven of you—in a *Bug?*"

"That's the idea," Dad said.

The attendant paused, then smiled. "Okay, where's the candid camera?" he asked.

"No, really," my dad responded.

But the gas station guy was now scanning the area, looking for the hidden van containing Allen Funt and the secret camera crew.

"Hey Larry!" he shouted to the cashier. "We're on *Candid Camera!*"

That got the attention of not only Larry, but everyone else within earshot. Heads peeked from car windows, pedestrians strolled our way, the mechanics sauntered over. We had quite a little audience as Mom led her line of little ducklings back from the bathroom and began wedging us back into the car.

There was obvious disappointment in the crowd when dad fired up the engine and began to roll out of the station with no hint of Allen Funt anywhere.

Dad thought the episode was highly amusing. Mom didn't

relish the attention nearly as much, which was really too bad when you consider this scene was basically repeated every time we stopped for gas, for food, for potty breaks, or to simply stretch our fourteen collective legs.

The amazing thing was that we actually survived this trip. We not only survived it, but had fun. We saw lots of the United States, we enjoyed a festival of fast food, we visited with aunts who immediately loved us and gave us cookies, and we got to play with our newfound cousins.

Thus, when I had kids of my own I decided we, too, needed to take a major road trip. My dad was elated to hear we were going to hit at least a portion of the historic Route 66.

"What are you going to drive?" he asked.

"Well, I was planning to drive our station wagon," I said.

"All four of you, crammed into that tiny thing?" he asked, shaking his head.

"It's a full-sized Ford Taurus wagon!" I protested.

He insisted we borrow his enormous Chevrolet "conversion" van, which contained a fold down bed, a sink, built in cabinets, and more floor space than a standard hotel room.

"The kids will travel so much better if they have some space," Dad said.

The interesting thing about sturdy Midwestern folks is that their entire philosophy about the way suffering builds character, of making do, and of frugality being next to godliness gets heaved right out the window once grandchildren enter the picture.

---

i still have a Volkswagen-shaped spine after all these years

Oh sure, suffering made sense for *me*. I still have a Volkswagen-shaped spine after all these years. Did *that* matter to him? But grandchildren were a completely different story.

So I took dad up on his offer, and we commenced on a journey that would ultimately take us through twelve states. We would overlook the Grand Canyon, cross the Rocky Mountains, enjoy some truly great steaks in Texas, tour the Eisenhower Presidential Library, and watch a fireworks show over the Mississippi River.

If our kids had any arguments about who was sitting too close to who, or who was breathing someone else's air, I never heard it. Sound can only travel so far. For all I know, they could have been playing soccer in the back of the 2,000-square-foot van.

If Dale and I ever have grandchildren who are poised to embark on a road trip, I have no doubt we'll do what we can to make it comfortable and wonderful for them. This is just a part of that whole "make things better for future generations" ideal that parents have been pursuing for thousands of years.

We all want our kids to have it better than we did.

That's a good impulse.

The weird part, and the difficult part, is that as life becomes more and more easy and comfortable it can also become more and more dangerous. I don't know if there's a correlation, but America is wealthier than ever before, and we have it easier than ever before, but kids seem to be at more risk than ever before. Much of the culture is in the toilet—drug and alcohol abuse is a massive problem for minors, teen pregnancy and abortion is widespread, and too many families are falling apart.

When we think in terms of making life better for the next

generation, it's clear that mere improvement in creature comforts isn't the gold standard to judge what we mean by "better."

It isn't really an "improvement" if we have widespread and affordable access to modern technology while our kids face widespread and profound moral disintegration.

Our kids need love and stability more than they need a computer. And they need the gospel more than they need all the other information you can pack into a DVD.

God wants our kids to have it better—as determined by Him.

If we let *Him* define what's good…it can't get any better than that.

Not Exactly a Cakewalk

It was a classic case of "failure to get the concept."

Our son's first grade class was putting on the back-to-school cakewalk, and Brad was beyond excited.

"Dad! Me and Mom are going to make a cake, and a bunch of other moms are going to make cakes, and then we get to walk on numbers on the floor, and when they call my number I get a free cake!"

"That sounds like fun," I said. "But you need to understand there's a component of chance in this game."

"I'll let other kids have a chance after I win!" Brad said.

"Now I have to go help Mom make a cake." He scampered to the kitchen.

I kept trying to gently explain there was no guarantee in this game. But Brad would simply shake his head and reply, "You'll see! And I'll even share with you and Mom and Mark."

---

there was enough **frosting** there to keep a dozen dentists **busy**

We arrived at the school and added Brad's German chocolate masterpiece to the festival of baked goods. There was enough frosting in that gymnasium to keep a dozen dentists busy for life.

"I'm going to win that one," Brad said, pointing to a cherry-topped Betty Crocker carbohydrate bomb.

The music started, the kids walked around the numbers, the music stopped and...Brad won. I blinked.

"Told ya," he said.

But the next round went to another kid. And that kid picked the cake Brad helped bake.

Brad looked up at me in dismay.

"That kid just took my cake," he whispered

"Well, he won," I said.

"But me and Mom made that cake! That's *my* cake!"

It took a loooonnnng time for me to convince Brad this wasn't an act of treacherous thievery that merited phoning the police.

In this life we truly don't get to have our cake and eat it, too. But if we follow Jesus, and store up treasures in heaven...when the music stops we can, indeed, have it all.

26

Happily Undevoted

If you're struggling to create a family devotional time that's both interesting and informative, nothing beats the strategy of having Max Lucado personally show up at your house to lead the session.

Regrettably, Max is often unavailable for this service, even if you beg him and pester him with relentless phone calls until he finally contacts the authorities. So, like it or not, you are probably on deck to lead the devotional time for your kids.

Many men, myself included, have found family devotional time to be a hugely daunting task, on a par with bull fighting or, more terrifying yet, hanging wallpaper with our spouse. This is especially true once your kids are old enough to have discovered video games and Mr. Incredible.

As my own boys, Mark and Brad, entered middle school, I remember asking myself, "How can I impart moral guidance to the same children who cackle hysterically and roll on the living room floor every time an advertisement comes on for Preparation H?"

But I plowed ahead, because spiritually leading my family is a calling from God. And He promises to be with us and to enable us as we seek to do the right thing.

If you start early in the life of your kids, devotions aren't actually all that hard. All you need is a Bible storybook with great pictures and you're basically set. You read the story, say prayers, and tuck them in. They adore this time with you, and they hang on your every word.

The only downside is that your kids will probably seize upon just one story that they find particularly fascinating, and they'll want you to read it over and over and over, day in and day out, until you can barely stand the thought of reading it one more time. You secretly begin rooting for the Philistines.

---

you **secretly** begin **rooting** for the Philistines

But enjoy the luxury of a Bible picture book while you can, because before you know it your kids will outgrow it, and you have to move to an entirely new level of depth and difficulty.

One day, armed with only my Bible and no artwork, I decided to do a devotion for Mark and Brad based on the story of David and Goliath. I wanted to teach them that if we trust in God, it's possible to overcome obstacles far bigger than ourselves.

What actually occurred, however, fell a tad short of the lesson goal.

I'd scarcely begun to outline the drama of the fateful battle when Brad posed a question.

"If Goliath came to our house, and if he really needed to use the bathroom, and if he needed to go number two, do you think our toilet would…"

I cut him off.

"All the giants are now dead, so we really don't have to confront that dilemma," I said, trying to dig back into the essential drama of the fateful battle.

But Brad merely shifted to another, almost identically unpleasant inquiry.

"Since Goliath was a giant, if he blew his nose, would his booger be the size of a golf ball?"

My other son, who's two years older and far more theologically astute, argued that it would be more the size of a pizza. They had a furious debate over what size of pizza it would be—small, medium, or large. This reminded them of how hungry they were, and could we please, please, please go to the pizza parlor?

We never finished the story of David and Goliath. Their Sunday school teacher said he would do it for me for twenty bucks.

But I kept slogging away at devotionals until it seemed we were all dreading it. Then I hit on a new strategy that really transformed the experience for all of us. I quit.

Seriously. I just quit. This may sound heretical. It may sound like I caved in. But I don't think so. Rather, I think I recognized that a routine devotional time no longer fit. The kids had outgrown it, just like they outgrew old clothes.

There's nothing very precise in the Bible about the practice we call family devotions. There are many calls to teach our children about God, but few specifics about filling this divine command. My view is that devotions make sense when your kids are younger and when you can hold their interest. It makes less sense if your kids interpret it as you treating them like they're still little.

If a planned family devotional time is still working in your situation, by all means keep it up. But in my case, when it just wasn't succeeding like it used to, instead of "doing a devotional"

I started taking my kids out to a burger place to just talk about God, life, school, the future, and other things.

They loved it. And I was no longer stressing about plowing through a lesson as my kids drifted into a coma. It was a win-win. And it seems to fit with the pattern that God outlined in Deuteronomy: "Fix these words of mine in your hearts and minds…. Teach them to your children, talking about them when you sit at home and when you walk along the road, when you lie down and when you get up" (Deuteronomy 11:18–19).

Mr. Lucado, you may have the night off.

27

Do the Math!

When my son Brad was in the fourth grade, I decided to help him hone his analytical skills by pointing out that five plus five equals whatever you want it to equal.

Brad stared at me and replied, "Five plus five is always ten."

"Not so fast," I said. "If a student thinks five plus five is nine, it might hurt his feelings if the teacher tells him he's wrong."

"So what?" Brad said, brow furrowed. "Five and five is always ten."

"We need to be sensitive about people's feelings," I said. "The main thing is whether they're sincere. If someone really believes five plus five is nine, we need to respect his opinion."

"Five and five is ten, period," he said. "This is stupid to even talk about."

"Brad, Brad, Brad," I replied, shaking my head. "Your problem is you're too narrow-minded. Something that's ten to you might be nine, or six, or even four to someone else. We can't be judging other people by our own views, especially if it makes other people feel bad. When a teacher asks a math question, the most important thing is that everyone in the class feels good about their answer."

"Five and five makes ten," Brad snapped, "no matter how anyone feels about it."

---

truth is **truth,** even if people don't **believe** it

"You're right," I told Brad. "I just wanted to drive home the point that truth is truth, even if people don't believe it. In our culture today, you're going to hear people saying truth is whatever you want it to be. Now they won't say this about five plus five, but they will say it about God."

And I reminded Brad that when Jesus said, "I am the way and the truth and the life," the issue isn't whether His words are "narrow," but whether they're true.

Keep in mind, mom and dad, that sometimes the best way to nuke a stupid idea is to simply ridicule it. Your kid will remember the lesson…and it's way more fun than a lecture.

Jesus Loves the Clueless Children, All the Clueless Children of the World

If you're a parent with a teenager living at home, you need to be aware that in most states it's still illegal to bury your child up to his neck in an anthill even if he REALLY gets on your nerves. I checked.

And while the Code of Federal Regulations doesn't specifically state that you cannot stick your teen in a crate and ship him to Bangladesh, your spouse will probably argue that this proposed action doesn't quite pass the "What Would Jesus Do" test. So you're still shot down.

As of the date of this writing, we have not one but TWO teenage boys occupying our home. The term "occupying" is used here in the same sense as when the German army was "occupying" Poland. My sons blitzkrieg the refrigerator, confiscate every towel in the house, requisition all the hot water, and then fire a barrage of dirty laundry while my wife and I plot ways to escape.

But that isn't the stuff that really bugs me. I mean, providing for our kids is a basic responsibility God gives me as a dad, and living with nominal amounts of teen debris comes with the territory of raising them.

What seriously gets to me is the fact that teenagers are—and I say this in a loving, caring, Christian manner—moronic.

Case in point: My wife was driving in busy downtown traffic a few years ago when she was horrified to find a teenager with a severe wisdom deficiency riding a motor scooter while holding a soda. For those of you who have no experience riding a two-wheeled vehicle, let me explain that in order to safely operate a scooter the rider needs to use both of his brain hemispheres. It also helps if he uses both hands, unless he's seeking to achieve the euphoric but brief sense of weightlessness that results from flying over the handlebars when only the front brake is applied. (This is called "applied physics," something that's covered in a high school science course which should be a mandatory requirement for scooter purchasers.)

My wife made several disparaging remarks about the lack of judgment exhibited by this particular teenage clueless person—as was her right as his mother.

Later that day, after I painstakingly and with robust volume explained the sheer folly of his actions, my son protested, "But how else could I keep my drink from spilling while I was riding?"

If this were the only example of moronicity in my teens, I could chalk it up to an aberration or a fluke or even gamma rays from the planet Zoobon. But this kind of stuff happens ALL THE TIME in my home.

Another case in point: As noted earlier, our youngest son, Brad, spent Christmas in the Intensive Care Unit of the local hospital when he was seventeen. I don't fault Brad for this. It wasn't his choice to have a ruptured appendix, and it wasn't his fault that the condition was initially misdiagnosed as the flu. Brad wasn't responsible for the subsequent infection, complications, and three weeks of hospitalization during which a team of dedicated health care specialists quite literally saved his life.

The one thing the doctors required was that Brad perform a daily series of breathing exercises intended to force air into his two partially collapsed lungs. After several attempts, Brad balked at the exercise because it was painful.

"I know it hurts," I said. "But three different experts with a combined medical expertise of more than a hundred years—the very doctors who saved your life—are saying you're at risk for pneumonia unless you do this exercise ten times per hour."

To which Brad replied, "What do they know?"

I won't go into detail regarding my response, other than to note that the hospital refused to release me from the restraints until I signed a document promising I wouldn't tie Brad into a human pretzel.

---

let me simply point out that ALL male teenagers are like this

---

Although I don't wish to generalize, let me simply point out that ALL male teenagers are like this, which makes me seriously question not only the wisdom of letting any of them vote, but also the wisdom of letting them out of their rooms before they're thirty.

But even if we could keep our teens locked in padded cells, the fact remains they would often exhibit the average IQ of dryer lint.

I would despair completely were it not for three facts:

FACT ONE: Fellow dads, you know that we were once *exactly* like them.

FACT TWO: God loves moronic, shallow, self-absorbed

people, and wants to transform them into wise, faithful, noble leaders of their homes and community.

FACT THREE: Fact Two also applies today to *us as dads*. Hopefully, we're further along on the journey of conformity to Christ, but we still have a loooonnnng way to go. Frankly, I think God deliberately programmed our teenagers the way they are just to give us, as fathers, a slight understanding of what we put Him through. Just as we do with God, teens can aggravate a father, defy a father, and even break a father's heart. But we love them still.

As Christian dads, we're generally pretty clear on the concept that God is using us to mold and shape our teens. We're less quick to understand that He's also using our teens to mold and shape us. In loving our kids, even in their often spectacular foolishness, we find our hearts beating in sync with a Father who always loves us.

29

Code Talkers

We handed the wrapped birthday present to our teenage son Brad and watched with anticipation as began to open it.

He extracted the sturdy "Relic" brand watch, stared at it for a moment, then murmured, "This is so sick."

I cringed. My wife and I had examined dozens of watches before selecting the one we felt Brad would most appreciate, though we couldn't really know if it would suit him. But for crying out loud, even if he didn't like it he didn't have to be so rude about…

Brad looked up at me with a broad grin.

"Sick means good, Dad."

"Sick is good?"

"This watch is totally sick, and it's exactly what I wanted," he replied.

I mused for a moment.

"Just so you know," I said, "I tried to get you a watch that was not only sick but violently ill, but your mother said we could only afford one that was slightly nauseous."

And I thought things were confusing enough a decade ago, back in the days when my boys used "bad" to describe something good (as in, "That Dodge Viper is so *bad!*")

---

i need a translator to understand my own offspring

I need a translator to understand my own offspring. But this is nothing new. Each generation of young people creates a new language, a series of code words identifying them as a cohort of the cool, as opposed to the gang of the geezers.

In my teenage days, shortly after the War of 1812, if something was good we called it "boss." This confused my mother, who was a teacher before she became a mom.

"That Corvette is so boss," I said one day.

"Boss? When did that become an adjective?"

"Mom, puh-leeze," I said, secretly thrilled that she was baffled.

"What happened to groovy?" she asked.

"*Groovy?*" I asked, appalled. "Only old people and mummies say groovy!"

"So groovy isn't 'with it' anymore?" she asked.

I was beginning to suffer from dangerously high levels of exposure to uncoolness, so I had to flee the room.

The worst thing was when my dad tried to speak to my friends using "our" language. Even if he managed (ever so briefly) to use a contemporary slang term in its proper context, it sounded so hokey coming out of his mouth.

"When I was your age we thought it was boss to say, 'Dig me daddy, I'm an Idaho spud!'" Dad beamed.

We all ran from the house lest we be infected with the dork-ification virus.

Because I can understand the impulse youngsters feel to have their own terminology, I've never made a fuss about it and I've never felt the need to fit in. But I've drawn one line in the sand.

One day I spied the following offensive bumper sticker on the back of a vehicle owned by a teenagerly person: "If Its Too Loud, Your Too Old!"

There was no way I could let that slide.

I spoke to the owner. "Listen up, my linguistically challenged little tot. If you're going to insult us older persons, at least have the decency to get your grammar right. If you're joining the term *it is* into the conjunction *it's,* then you need an apostrophe between the 't' and the 's.' That same rule applies to your misuse of the word *your* which is actually supposed to be *you're,* as in 'You're too old.' Got it?"

"Dude, like, I didn't understand a word you just said," he replied.

"That's because we old people have our own little code language, which we refer to as 'English.' You'd better master it if you want a bad job some day."

"Huh?"

"And a final word of advice: If you don't want to humiliate yourself in your English class, make sure you don't let your participles dangle."

He was checking his zipper when I left him.

An amazing thing about language is that even with all the twists, turns, fads, and generational codes, I'm reading the same Bible as the row of teenagers who sit across from me week after week in church. And the timeless Word of God is speaking clearly and powerfully to all of us, whether we're wearing sandals or burgundy wing-tipped shoes.

Is this sick, or what?

Who Designated This Driver?

The fact that teenagers can legally drive proves one of three things:

(1) Your state legislators hate you; or

(2) Your state legislators use illegal drugs; or

(3) Your legislators use illegal drugs *and* hate you.

What other explanation can there possibly be? How could any sober and benevolent group of lawmakers decide, "Hey!

Let's allow teenagers to get behind the wheel of what's basically a 2,000-pound bomb on wheels! Let's pass a law enabling them to whiz by us mere feet apart on a two-lane road even though we know they'll be looking in the rearview mirror to ensure that each of their individually combed hairs is still in place."

---

the minimum driving age should be thirty-two

I think the minimum driving age should be thirty-two. Wouldn't you feel a whole lot safer if you knew every driver on the road was alive while Richard Nixon was president?

I certainly would.

In my state, not only does the vehicle code allow children to get a "learner's permit" while they're still essentially toddlers, but the law specifically states that these youthful drivers must have a few dozen practice hours with a "responsible adult," which is nothing more than a thinly veiled euphemism for "dad or mom."

Yes, fellow parents, the people YOU voted into office have retaliated by giving your teenagers a full legal right to pester you and beg and whine and complain and nag and caterwaul and fuss and snivel until you agree to teach them to drive. Without a fair trial, you've been summarily sentenced to forty hours of hard time. Remember this the next time you go to the polls.

And don't harbor any pitiful hope that your child is in the dark about his auto-related legal rights. Even if your child isn't an exceptional student, even if your child flunks a history quiz because he thought the War of 1812 began in 1942, even if your child cannot even memorize the first three words of the U.S. Constitution, he can quote verbatim the entire section of the state code that allows him to drive.

So it was that I found myself swallowing hard as I buckled myself into the passenger seat and handed the keys to my son Mark.

"Before you start the car," I said, "repeat back the rules."

Mark took a deep breath. "Before I start the car, I buckle my seatbelt and adjust the mirrors," he recited. "Before I back up, I always look in my rear view mirrors. Before turning, I always use my turn signals."

"And what else?"

Mark frowned.

"I don't remember any other rules," he said.

"The big one—Thou shalt not race the car in an irresponsible teenagerly manner and lose control and plow into a big rig on the freeway and thereby envelop your beloved father in a raging fireball of exploding debris, or you're grounded for a month. Repeat it."

"I'll obey the speed limits," he said.

"Close enough," I replied.

Just to let Mark get a feel for the car, we began our lesson in a large, empty parking lot.

"The interplay of the clutch and the gas pedal is usually the hardest part for a new driver to learn," I instructed. "Just slowly give it gas as you ease your foot off the clutch."

The car lurched forward a couple feet and the engine died.

"Sorry!" Mark said.

"No sweat. You didn't hurt anything. Just give it a little more gas next time," I advised.

The main trouble with the phrase "a little more gas" is that it's somewhat imprecise.

The engine screamed as the RPM needle kissed the red line. The steel-belted Michelin radials spun like twin buzz saws, carving deep ruts into the asphalt. My head snapped deeply into the headrest. We rocketed through the parking lot as the G forces flattened my corpuscles into tiny little bio-pancakes.

"BRRRAAAAAAAAAAAAAAKE!" I shrieked, nearly committing a hygienic lapse.

Mark stood on the brake pedal with both feet, laying out a skid trail longer than a regulation basketball court.

"Awesome!" he exclaimed as we shuddered to a stop.

Our first lesson, while brief, was nevertheless a success (with "success" defined as "we lived through it.")

In each succeeding lesson, Mark got better and more confident. The day finally came for him to take his driver test and obtain a real license.

As he walked into the motor vehicle office, I mentally bid farewell to his childhood. The boy God gave me was becoming a man. It had all happened so fast.

Next to me, in the same boat, stood another dad with misty eyes. I turned to him. "Hard to have them grow up," I gulped.

He choked. "The insurance is two thousand bucks a year," he said.

Suddenly we were both weeping.

31

Don't Touch That Pie!

One thing I look forward to each Thanksgiving is my mom's traditional pumpkin pie. Ever since I was a kid, my mom has produced—with unvarying precision—a culinary work of majesty that's made even more wonderful by the fact that she exactly replicates the feat decade after decade.

But last Thanksgiving she decided, quite inexplicably, to change it.

She might just as well have tried to "improve" my grandfather's venerable pocket watch by making it digital. Oy! "What have you done?" I moaned to her. "The filling is light and fluffy! It's supposed to be heavy and dense!"

"Like you?" asked my oldest son, Mark.

I chased him around the couch a few times but he eventually bolted from the room and ran laughing down the street. Fortunately, I'd already shrewdly passed my genes to him when he was but an embryo, so I have the satisfaction of knowing he'll one day be as portly and balding as I am.

I made my way back toward the kitchen to continue my conversation with my mom, but my wife interrupted me.

"Don't complain," she whispered. "The pie is still wonderful, and you don't want to hurt her feelings."

---

i was **trying** to show her the **error** of her ways

"I'm not complaining; I'm trying to help her see the error of her ways," I said.

"You've been sniveling, whining, fussing, fretting, and griping," my wife countered.

"But that's different from actually complaining," I noted.

In addition to passing on favorite family foods from generation to generation, I'm also trying to pass on the habit of thankfulness. Although the Bible never says we have to be thankful *for* everything that happens, it does teach us to be thankful *in* all things. Simply thanking God for who He is can be a transformative experience, even in hard circumstances. Thankfulness re-orients our attitude.

Someday, I may even manage to be thankful for smarty-pants teenagers.

32

Driving Ambition

I heard the words, but the message was so bizarre that my mind refused to believe what my ears were communicating.

I stared at my sixteen-year-old son, Brad.

"Could you take it from the top on that one?" I asked.

So he took a deep breath.

"Well, since I have my license now, we're short one car. So I was thinking that maybe if you bought a new Escalade, it would solve all kinds of problems, cuz, like, you know how sometimes you take business trips into the mountains and it's, like, snowing, then you would have four-wheel drive and it would be safer, plus we would have an extra set of wheels. But since me and my friends go snowboarding all the time, I could, like, sort of always drive it and then you wouldn't have to take me to school in the morning. But when you were, you know, going to the mountains, then you could, like, borrow it for the day. But just try not to do it too often."

"Let me see if I grasp the deal," I replied. "I buy a new Cadillac SUV that costs as much as the gross domestic product of Peru, and it effectively becomes your vehicle, but I can borrow it on rare occasions as long as it doesn't terribly inconvenience you. Is that it?"

---

he said i **always** make things sound so **negative**

"You always make things sound so negative," Brad said.

Because I'm a kind and compassionate father who ultimately wants his children to be happy, I gave Brad a major gift. I answered no to his request. Instead I bought myself a more comfortable car, and I let him use my old 1990 Nissan.

One of the worst things a dad can do is pander to the insane whims of his teenager. Choosing wisdom is better than choosing popularity. And as a bonus, wisdom is often cheaper.

33

Wait a Minute, Mr. Postman!

The package arrived at the United States Capitol and was routed for routine screening. The x-ray image that lit up the monitor stopped the technician cold. The package was filled with a mishmash of electrical wires connected to multiple boxes.

At once the package was carefully moved to a safe location, and the Capitol Hill bomb squad was called in.

The plain brown box contained a return address and was therefore swiftly traced back to the sender.

Um, me.

I hadn't meant to alarm anyone. I work for a Congressman, and over the course of a few years, as he replaced his bulky cell phones with newer models, I found myself in possession of all kinds of outdated battery chargers and adapters. They were cluttering up my office in his home district in California.

So one day I just crammed them all into a box and shipped the stuff back to the Congressman's Washington office so they could be inventoried or tossed.

And thus one day I got the Phone Call.

It was Pam, the Congressman's personal assistant.

"Dave, did you mail us a package full of wires?"

"Yep," I said. "Have fun sorting it all out."

the **bomb** squad was **not** amused

"The bomb squad was not amused," she said. "Especially after discovering they had wasted their morning preparing to defuse three Motorola cell phone chargers."

Yikes!

The only thing that saved my bacon was my intent. Had I done it as a prank or a threat, I probably would have been carted off to the slammer for an exciting new career in license plate production. Fortunately, there's no law against cluelessness.

Sometimes, in our role as a spouse or parent, we do incredibly clueless, stupid things. We forget the important dinner engagement, the anniversary, or the school play. But there's a world of difference between an unintended error and a malicious act. If I step on your toe by accident, I would apologize and you would quickly forgive me. If I stepped on your toe on purpose, you might deck me.

Whenever you do something utterly clueless in your family, and there was no bad intent, make sure you explain everything to your spouse or kids. Understanding your intent makes all the difference in the world when you want someone to forgive you.

Just ask the bomb squad.

34

Midnight Musings

I'm lying in a bed that isn't my own, in a room cluttered with the debris of someone else's childhood. Boy Scout memorabilia.

T-shirts. And inside the closet (its door was open when I entered the room), an entire collection of Teenage Mutant Ninja Turtles on a top shelf.

I'm away from home on business, overnighting at a friend's home instead of the Holiday Inn. The room with toys is vacant because the child is gone.

I can't stop gazing into the closet. It has sucked me into a time warp. A mere decade ago my boys used to play in this room, in this house, on this quiet street. They played with the boy who owned the ugly Mutant Turtle action figures. Dayne owned the toys. Dayne wore the Boy Scout uniform. Dayne plastered the bunk bed with stickers.

I can see him still as I stare at his toys. Blonde, skinny kid with a ready laugh. How on earth is it possible that Dayne— this little boy whose bed I'm borrowing for the night—has been whisked away and transformed into a soldier? Does the Army have any clue he still has all his toys stashed away? Does the Pentagon realize they've handed a machine gun to a kid?

I blink. I shake my head.

I remind myself that Dayne isn't a kid anymore. I moved away, and he grew up. He became an Eagle Scout.

When he graduated from high school he told his parents he was going to join the Army and protect his country. Then he saw the Twin Towers go down. Everything changed, for all of us.

His mom and dad, Becky and Scott, were torn between pride and fear.

"Dayne! People will try to shoot you!" exclaimed his mom.

Dayne replied, "Mom, I'll just shoot them first."

His dad asked Dayne if he'd really stopped to think through the decision.

"Dad," Dayne replied, "this country has given me so much. I have to do this."

Later, recalling the conversation, Scott looked at me—blinking back tears—and said, "How could I possibly say anything against that?"

Boot camp was awful, as it always is for everyone. But Dayne hung in there. He did well. His aim was so true they canceled a remaining session of his target practice and let him call home while the other recruits learned to handle a weapon. Dayne has a leg up; he has hunted his entire life.

In the group photo of young, stern soldiers looking at the camera, one face stands out. It's Dayne, the only guy smiling from ear to ear. His sergeant dubs him "Sunshine." It's a ribbing, not an insult. Dayne is irrepressibly happy about his chance to protect the folks back home. Folks like me and my family.

Dayne wanted to do something important and gutsy, right in the face of the enemy. So he found himself on a helicopter in Iraq, doing his part to topple the mad regime of Saddam Hussein.

Dale and I are proud of this little boy who has grown into an awesome young man. We support his mission. We support his Commander in Chief. We pray that worldwide terrorism can be vanquished. We also pray that Dayne can come home soon, get married, and have sons who can play with the Mutant Turtle toys. (His future daughters deserve some normal dolls.)

In any war, some of our soldiers—only God knows the number—will not come home. We know that. Dayne's parents know that. It's a fact of war. But the alternative—letting the madmen, dictators, suicide bombers, and sociopaths dominate the world—is simply unacceptable. So, fearful and yet proud,

Scott and Becky bid their son Godspeed and sent him off to war.

As I drifted off to sleep in Dayne's bed, I prayed for the boy-turned-soldier.

Dale and I have prayed for him together many times. Praying is the least we can do…as well as the most.

PART 3

Dude Awakening
A Man and His Faith...
in Today's World

35

The Great "Designated Driver" Adventure

Ed glanced at me nervously as the Secret Service agent outlined our duties as drivers.

And judging from the increasing width of Ed's eyes while the agent explained the scenarios in which we could lose our lives, I knew I'd stretched the limits of our friendship.

Ed was a junior high school teacher, and I was a writer of memos and press releases. Normally, the gravest danger we faced in our day jobs involved Microsoft programs that periodically emitted scary yellow triangles with exclamation marks inside. But I had plunged us into a completely different world. For one night, we were official drivers for the "press pool" that followed Very Important Candidates every four years.

"The Protectee will be in the white sedan," the agent said. "If the car containing the Protectee is fired upon, we will accelerate at a high rate of speed. Do not attempt to follow us at a high rate of speed. If you attempt to follow us at a high rate of speed, you may be fired upon."

Fired upon?

By the good guys?

On purpose?

Ed stared at me.

I really needed to use the restroom.

"The only vehicles on the road," the agent continued, "will

be the motorcade and the Highway Patrol. However, do not change lanes unless the lead vehicle changes lanes. Patrol cars will be passing you at extreme rates of speed. If you change lanes, you risk having your van plowed into by a patrol car. Any questions thus far?"

I wanted to revisit the whole "you may be fired upon" issue, but I figured the greatest immediate threat to my bodily person was Ed. And reminding Ed about the potential of friendly fire didn't seem particularly prudent.

We weren't even being paid for this gig. I'd roped Ed into the deal by pointing out we would get a free photo of ourselves standing with the Very Important Candidate. It would be both historic and educational.

---

i **tried** to tell him several times it **would** be fun

Plus, as I tried to tell him several times, it would be fun.

And it would be, as long as no one shot us or rammed our van at 120 miles per hour, thereby turning our vehicle into a raging fireball full of hostile press persons.

We walked to our vehicles, took our seats behind the wheel, and began the exciting task of sitting and waiting. And waiting. And waiting some more.

The Very Important Jet finally landed, releasing the Protectee and a herd of media folks. Scores of uniformed officers were joined by scores of athletic, civilian-clothed persons who looked no different than the average yuppie with a hearing aid and a moderately concealed Uzi.

The press pool mashed themselves into our vans and we took off, following at the assigned distance, knuckles white as patrol cars roared past us like cruise missiles.

The Protectee was driven to a college gymnasium packed with an enthusiastic crowd. He gave a stirring and inspiring speech—at least, we assumed it was stirring and inspiring, based on the applause we heard in the distance. Ed and I missed the actual speech, as we were under strict orders to stay with our vehicles and issue a caterwaul of protest if anyone attempted to hand us a ticking briefcase.

The rally ended, the press herd mooed its way back into our vans, and we returned to the airport.

As the press trampled its way back into the plane, someone called out words that are still frozen into the core of my brain: *"We need to shoot the drivers."*

I was going to hurl myself to the tarmac and beg for mercy when I saw a campaign staffer organizing a group photo in front of the jet. I scrambled out of my van and joined Ed in meeting the Protectee, who shook our hands and thanked us while the camera flashed.

"I'll mail you each a photo," said the photographer. Then she boarded the plane.

On the first Tuesday of the following November, the Very Important Candidate lost.

Our photo never showed up.

I bought a substitute thank you gift for Ed. A coffee mug. I hope he cherishes it. I'm afraid to ask.

Because I'm an aide to a Congressman, I periodically have the opportunity to brush up against a Senator here, a Governor there, and even the occasional cabinet official. But I'm far from an "insider." Drivers are not insiders. After watching scores of public figures, I can tell you that the true, ultimate insiders are the people with maximum access to the person in power.

And that's why it's so stunning to me to read a Bible passage telling me I may "approach the throne of grace with confidence" (Hebrews 4:16).

God has no staff; He has *sons*. That's me and you—and anyone who has been adopted into God's family through faith in Jesus Christ. With God, we're always allowed inside to His presence; we never get stuck standing out by the car.

Talk about maximum access to the Person in Power!

Just Breathe!

It was foolhardy, it was dangerous, and it broke all the rules of diving. But there I was, submerged in thirty feet of water off the coast of Molokini, a tiny island off the coast of Maui. The rest of the group was on the other side of the island. I was utterly alone, stupidly alone, and something big had just brushed against the side of my face.

I was more startled than alarmed. I turned to get a better look, but not fast enough to see what was coming. And then the thing lunged at me.

Unbelievably, I was being attacked by a massive squid. Before I could even begin to react, it latched its tentacles over my head and ripped off my mask. Its probing appendages clutched at my face again and again until I woke in my bed and yelled, "Gaaaaahhh! What are you doing to my nose?"

"Oh, I didn't mean to wake you," my wife replied.

But she kept her squid hold on my nostrils.

"What are you DOING???!!!!" I yelped.

"You were snoring, so I was trying to put a Breathe Right on your nose," she said. "Stop squirming."

In case you aren't familiar with the product known as Breathe Right, it's an ingenious device that adheres to your nose and flares your nostrils in order to improve airflow. (A notable side effect is that the Breathe Right makes you look remarkably like an angry bull, which is why football players don't mind wearing them during a game, but you never see fashion models sporting them.)

"Why didn't you just wake me up and ask me to put it on myself?" I asked Dale.

"I didn't want to bother you," she said.

"Bother me?" I replied. "Did it bother Captain Nemo to fight off the sea beast? For crying out loud, I was so terrified I ripped my pillow in half!"

"Well, at least the Breathe Right is on now so you'll stop snoring and we can get some rest," she answered. "Just sweep up the feathers in the morning." She turned off the lamp and pulled up the covers.

She went right to sleep. I, meanwhile, stared up at the dark ceiling and waited for the adrenaline spigot to turn off. I think it took me an hour to nod off, and my subsequent dreams were punctuated by visions of a giant Hoovermatic vacuum cleaner assailing my schnozzle.

The maddening thing about this ordeal is that I don't even snore. I may occasionally perform a mild sniff or a moderate snort, but certainly nothing along the lines of actual snoring. If I made a racket that was anything approaching the nasal fanfare of which Dale accuses me, I would certainly hear it. But I sleep just fine. Once my head hits that pillow, I doze like a slowly decomposing log. It isn't my fault Dale is a light sleeper.

When morning dawned, I was still shaken by the night's events.

"Dale, I know you meant well, but you pretty much ruined my sleep last night. In the future, it would be better to just ignore any of my nominal and infrequent breathing irregularities," I advised.

"Nominal and infrequent breathing irregularities?" she replied. "Dave, you sounded like a Husqvarna chain saw. I endured it as long as I could."

i smiled at her in my typically patient manner

I smiled at her in my typically patient manner. "Dale, Dale, Dale. Let's not make a rhetorical mountain over the small molehill of a slight sound in the night," I said.

Dale folded her arms and rolled her eyes, which isn't the standard nonverbal cue to indicate agreement. "Dave, you sound like a train wreck. Like a jackhammer. Like a demolition crew. Without your Breathe Right on, it's like I'm sleeping next to a backfiring truck engine. The fact that you sleep right through it doesn't mean it isn't happening. Good grief, after all the complaining you've done about your college roommates, you should be the last one to question whether a snoring person can sleep through his own noise."

"But that was different," I said. "You can't compare me to Tim or Brian. Tim had nocturnal deafness. You could have set off an air raid siren right next to him and he wouldn't have even twitched. And Brian was comatose when he slept. His corpuscles literally ceased functioning at night. But he snored like a rhino, and the vibrations actually knocked books off the shelves."

"And you're just like both of them," Dale said. "Will you just trust me on this?"

Ahhhh. The sixty-four-billion-dollar question: *Will you trust me?*

(Pause for a moment while Dave switches into serious philosophical mode.)

That question of trust is at the heart of all significant relationships. Trust isn't something you give willy-nilly unless you want to get burned. Trust is something earned by a host of actions that build confidence.

Do I trust my longtime mechanic when he calls me and says, "No, the battery was fine. You need a new starter, and it's going to be expensive."

Do I trust my doctor when he tells me he has found a cancerous mass, and he needs to operate at once?

Do I trust my best friend when he tells me I'm flat wrong about something in which I feel justified?

To trust is to have faith in the motivation of another. To trust is to defer to the wisdom of another. To trust is to assume that the person asking for trust is worthy of your confidence.

Trust is really synonymous with faith. Faith isn't required when everything is just as clear as a polished window. Faith is exercised when things are murky, blurred, or flat-out black.

Do I trust Dale? Of course I do. And I trust her about issues far more serious than snoring, which, based on her testimony, I believe I perform at a volume that's sufficient to send small animals scurrying in panic to their burrows—*even though I've never heard it.*

I trust her when she points out my blind spots. (If I could see them, they wouldn't be called "blind spots," would they?)

I trust Dale has my best interests at heart, because she has a track record of trustworthiness spanning decades.

---

a spouse who loves you **deeply** can still be **wrong**

Now, the problem with trusting people—even people who have your best interests at heart—is that they can be wrong. Doctors aren't infallible. A mechanic can miss a loose wire and misdiagnose your engine problem. A well-meaning friend may have bad information or suffer from his own misperception. A spouse who loves you deeply can still be wrong about something. Yet, even with their flaws and limitations, we put our faith in other people every day. We have to. We can't function in life without trusting others.

When we deal with God, the issue of trust goes to an entirely new level.

The question He poses is the same question we hear from mere mortals: "Will you trust Me?"

But in this case, there are no limitations on the person asking us to trust. God doesn't suffer from bad information, or a misperception. He isn't fallible. His motivation is always pure and His wisdom is unbounded. He has zero flaws. He's incapable of lacking integrity.

And, importantly, His past performance on our behalf has earned our confidence. The cross of Christ doesn't answer all our questions, but it answers enough of them. God has earned our trust.

The suffering of Jesus doesn't explain my own suffering, but His sacrifice should forever put to rest the question of whether He loves me.

The Incarnation speaks to His willingness to enter our painful world, the Cross speaks to the depth of His commitment to our eternal well-being, and the Resurrection assures us He's powerful enough to conquer not only His own grave, but ours as well.

Hordes of questions nevertheless remain. Painful, traumatic, burning questions that can leave us reeling. In the dark of the night, they can make us question whether God indeed loves us, or whether there's even a God at all. Why did that young mother, so full of life and so beloved by her family, get killed by a drunk driver? Why did God allow that child to be so horribly abused for all those years? Why is my child confined to a wheelchair? Why, after I prayed my heart out, did my spouse walk out on me? Since God is all-powerful, why won't He just fix the mess I'm in?

The questions pour out with our tears, and there are no ready answers.

And God is still beckoning to us, asking us the same question.

"Will you trust Me?"

Had He not sent Jesus, my answer would be an emphatic "No way! Life brims with tragedy and pain, and You are insulated from all of it!"

But with the cross, God has silenced the allegation that He's distant from our pain or removed from our lives. In the Cross we see God Himself taking the form of humanity and living with us, dying for us, and rising with a promise to return and one day wipe away every tear from our eyes.

Yes, I can trust Him.

I still periodically panic, lose my way, lash out in confusion, and drop into a funk.

But I keep coming back, because He has earned my faith.

The Cross is the ultimate answer to every question that haunts you.

Will you trust Him on this?

37
Snake Eyes

I stood in a loose circle with five of my best friends as we stared at the prized possession. We were in a state of hushed awe. The possibilities were simply endless.

Kevin's dad had killed a massive rattlesnake earlier in the day, whacking off its head with a garden hoe and dumping the carcass in a trash can.

In our rural community it wasn't all that rare for snakes to show up, searching for water and a patch of shade when the weather turned hot. But this was a particularly large and impressive specimen. And Kevin's dad had simply tossed it in the trash—one more of the many bizarre things we kids just didn't understand about adults. *We* wouldn't have thrown away a perfectly good dead snake in almost mint condition any more than our parents would have flushed England's Crown Jewels down the toilet. I mean, this snake had a set of rattles the size of a corncob. This was beyond cool; this was totally boss!

So we took the first opportunity to retrieve the carcass from the trash.

"Whaddya wanna do with it first?" asked Matt.

"Let's freak someone out," replied Danny.

We lugged the dearly departed down the street until we came to a section of sidewalk bordering some overgrown shrubs. Then we laid the body out on the sidewalk in an impressive "S" shape and concealed the headless section under the bushes. Then we waited until a car came into view.

To our delight, the driver was a woman in her fifties, cruising through the subdivision in her enormous Sedan DeVille. On cue, and doing our best to appear distraught, we began hopping up and down and pointing at the snake.

The car slowed to a stop, and the woman pressed the button to roll down the front passenger window.

"Now what are you kids having a fuss…" Her voice trailed off as she saw the distinctive diamond-pattern on the snake's body. The color in her face quickly drained.

"Get away from that snake!" she screamed.

"You mean this one?" Kevin asked as he reached down,

grabbed the dead reptile, and shook it in such a manner that it appeared to be quite alive.

The poor woman nearly swooned. Her face got all blotchy and her hands went all wobbly.

We suddenly felt rather bad.

"Better let her know it isn't alive," I said.

Kevin walked toward the car, calling out, "Don't worry, there ain't anything to fear."

But the woman looked fearful indeed. She looked beyond fearful. She looked like a 3-D version of that famous *The Scream* painting that you study in college art textbooks.

"Look!" Kevin continued, thrusting his hand into the cabin of the car to offer the woman a close-up view of the expired serpent. "There's nothing to be scared of. The head's clean off."

Strangely, she did not find this information to be soothing. She shrieked, punched the accelerator, and roared down the road.

We truly felt bad about causing such alarm, and we seriously discussed the option of dumping the expired viper back in the trash. But we quickly recovered our wits, then tried several additional versions of our gag, including one episode where we had Brian lay on the ground and clutch his leg and wail, just to add a further dash of drama.

It all ended too soon when a neighbor called Kevin's mom and filled her in about our lively street theater production.

Sadly, Kevin's mom had no formal training as a critic of the performing arts, so her review was excessively and unjustly negative. Suffice it to say the show was shut down after opening day. Which was just as well, since all of us actors were grounded and wouldn't have been able to show up anyway.

As I grew up, and even into my high school years, I continued to be a big fan of dead snakes. A friend of mine had a Volkswagen Bug, which turned out to be the perfect vehicle to utilize for a sport called "snake popping." In the fall months, toward dusk, three or four of us would pile into the car and drive a few miles west of town in search of rattlers basking in the sun-kissed warmth of the pavement.

There was a fairly precise science to snake popping. First you had to drive slowly, peering down the road with eagle vision, locating a dozing snake without alarming it so that it slithered off safely into the grass.

Once located, you couldn't simply run over the snake at high speed. You had to go fast but also precisely time your approach so you could slam on the brakes and still be skidding as the tires reached the body of the ill-fated serpent. Only this technique constituted actual snake popping. The friction was a crucial element. To hear a mere "thump-thump" sound as the tires rolled over the snake was the equivalent of striking out with all the bases loaded.

The effort was scored on both style and substance, with highest marks reserved for a snake popped closest to the middle of the skid trail. Bonus points were added for a head shot.

In case you haven't yet figured it out, I hate rattlesnakes. I don't simply fear them. I have a visceral loathing for them.

I realize rattlesnakes are a part of the natural ecosystem, but so is the bird flu virus, and I'm not too fond of that either. So if you're an ecosystem activist, you can save your letters; I already know rattlesnakes are critical to controlling the rodent population, and I know they serve an important function in nature, and I know they aren't after me, and I know my fears are irrational. I, nevertheless, still hate rattlesnakes. This is an emotional reaction, and you aren't going to be able to talk me out of it.

The neighborhood where I live is adjacent to a large expanse of oak and manzanita "open space," and I know snakes live there. Snakes are my neighbors. I'm just saying that if one of these neighbors ever stops by to visit, perhaps to borrow a cup of sugar, they're going to go home sugarless and also a few ounces lighter in the head department.

The teenage guys who invited me to go on my first snake popping adventure also happened to be sincere followers of Jesus, and so they invited me to a Bible study. I had never before been to a Bible study. I'd been to religious training and Sunday services and Holy Days of Obligation and mandatory catechism classes, but never to a Bible study conducted by and for teenagers. And they did it voluntarily. It was their idea. No adults were involved.

In a way, it sounded kind of odd. I mean, snake popping made all the sense in the world. It was fun, and it helped reduce the poisonous snake population. But why would these otherwise completely normal, fun-loving guys want to have a Bible study when it wasn't obligatory?

But I went, because they'd befriended me. So I guess you could technically put snake popping into the category of "outreach ministry." It worked for me. [NOTE TO YOUTH PASTORS: You may want to run this concept by the Church Board before you go out and buy a Volkswagen for this purpose.

You know how uptight Church Board members can be.]

When I look back on the road that led me to a personal relationship with Christ, I see lying there the body of a pulverized snake.

And when you think about it...the same is true for all Christians.

The book of Genesis records the spiritual fall of man, a fall in which a crafty serpent was the catalyst. It was the serpent who called into question the trustworthiness of God, and who tempted Adam and Eve to break faith with their Creator. God therefore pronounced a curse upon the serpent: "Because you have done this, cursed are you above all the livestock and all the wild animals! You will crawl on your belly and you will eat dust all the days of your life" (Genesis 3:14).

God went on to make a prophetic utterance: Adam and Eve would produce descendants, and "enmity" would exist between their offspring and the serpent. God also explained that this state of conflict would culminate in an event in which the serpent would "strike the heel" of a certain man—but that man would also "crush" the serpent's head (Genesis 3:15).

The death and resurrection of Jesus constitutes a snake-popping of truly cosmic proportions. The snake body is still wriggling in its death throes, but at some point God is going to scrape that creature off the road and toss him into the burn barrel.

And I get to watch!

Oh man, it doesn't get any better than this.

38

Attack of the Techno-Dork

The conversation went exactly like this:

ME: "My e-mail isn't working."

TECH SUPPORT GUY: "Let me trouble-shoot it for you. First, what operating system are you using?"

ME: "I have no idea."

TECH SUPPORT GUY: (Pause.) "Okaaay. What e-mail program do you use?"

ME: "I have no idea."

TECH SUPPORT GUY: "What kind of connection do you use?"

ME: "I have no idea."

TECH SUPPORT GUY: "Are you serious?"

ME: "Yes."

TECH SUPPORT GUY: "Um, how about if I just Timbuktu into your computer and look at it from this end?"

ME: "Feel free. Go with your emotions. I won't stand in your way."

TECH SUPPORT GUY: "Okay. So go ahead and open Timbuktu and I'll take it from there."

ME: "I have no idea how to do that."

TECH SUPPORT GUY: (Long pause.) "Do you know what Timbuktu is?"

ME: "I believe it's a small town in the middle of nowhere."

TECH SUPPORT GUY: "What's your user name?"

ME: "I have no idea."

TECH SUPPORT GUY: "How do you log on?"

ME: "I don't. I just always leave everything on and hope nothing changes. But every once in a while something goes wrong, and then I call this number and humiliate myself by talking to someone like you."

TECH SUPPORT GUY: (Very long pause.) "This is, like, a joke? Right? Like one of those quality control monitoring exercises to make sure I'm patient and courteous no matter how dense the caller is?"

Sadly, it wasn't a practical joke. I started my current job back in the days when computers had small green screens chiseled out of solid granite. We used these computers as word processors, and we believed the absolute height of technology was the ability to cut and paste text on-screen.

When we heard rumors one day that someone in our building had obtained a computer that could show a picture on the screen, our whole office was in awe in much the same way a Stone Age tribe might react to amazing stories of microwave ovens or Thighmasters.

Because 97 percent of my job consisted of writing letters, memos, and reports, I never really kept up with the exploding technology. When our office manager introduced us to the concept of e-mail, I asked, "Why would I take the time to type out a note when I can just pick up the phone?" To me, e-mail seemed about as sensible as tapping out messages on a telegraph or sending smoke signals.

---

i was immediately pounded by the **cruel** tsunami of **progress**

But everyone said the Internet thing was the wave of the future, so I flopped my pudgy body on the surfboard of technology and paddled cautiously into the digital sea, where I was immediately pounded by the cruel tsunami of progress. I did manage to learn how to send e-mail, but that was about it.

It was irritating enough to have to use the Internet at work, but my two boys were begging me incessantly to get service at home so they could do research for school projects.

"Why not just use our set of encyclopedias?" I asked.

Brad's face went white.

"Only Amish people use encyclopedias! I'll get laughed out of school if we don't have the Internet!"

Mark was equally adamant.

"Dad, being without the Internet is like not having indoor plumbing! I can't even chat with my friends!"

"Let's not go overboard, Mark. You were just chatting with Kyle when I picked you up from school," I replied.

Mark rolled his eyes.

"I was *talking* with Kyle! Chatting is something you do on the computer!"

From that point the conversation became utterly incoherent as the boys used scary words like "download speeds" and "DSL" and "megabytes" and "gigahertzes" and "corpuscles" and "defribulators."

152

To be honest, sometimes I feel obsolete. Technologically speaking, I'm a rusty antique you'd find covered in spider webs and pigeon poop in the corner of a ramshackle barn.

But the Bible says I'm also a new creation in Christ—that the old has gone and the new has come. Ultimately, all the gizmos and gadgets will pass into oblivion...yet I will still forever be a new creation. A redeemed soul is never obsolete.

My kids, however, still need some convincing.

ME: "Hey, when I hit the button for the D drive, the cup holder came out. What does that mean?"

BRAD: "It means God wants you to be Amish."

He may be right...

This Job Bombs!

On the worst day of my worst job, I had to carry a canister of nitroglycerin up a long flight of stairs.

The explosive liquid had been mixed with a thickening agent that looked like soggy graham crackers. A co-worker assured me it wouldn't detonate, even if I jiggled it. Still, I noticed *he* hadn't volunteered to carry it.

Fresh out of high school, I'd landed a job on a steam drilling rig. A steam drilling rig is pretty much the same thing as an oil drilling rig—the major difference being that instead of seeking "black gold" we were on a quest for "white hissing vapor," which is why Hollywood makes no movies about it.

John Wayne once did a great movie called *The Hellfighters* about a crew of tough guys who would bravely advance on a flaming gusher of oil and snuff out the raging inferno while hot black oil rained down upon them. MGM considered doing a sequel featuring John Wayne in a field of steam drilling rigs, but he balked when he found out his main line consisted of, "Men, it looks like that well is about to emit a wisp of white vapor!"

Our steam drilling work was, nevertheless, complex and dangerous. Employing the same equipment used to drill miles into the earth to reach oil, we were drilling for heat that would be converted into electricity.

Here's the short version of how it worked: We attached a gargantuan drill bit to a length of pipe, which we would then spin into the earth. When the "stand" of pipe was drilled down as far as possible, we attached another length of pipe and continued the process. By attaching length after length of pipe, we could drill miles into the ground.

One day a mile-long stand of pipe got badly stuck when we were pulling it up to change the drill bit. We spent hours trying to free it up, but it was hopeless. So we decided to cut our losses and send down an explosive charge at the "kink" in order to retrieve as much pipe as possible. The idea was to twist the pipe in the "unscrew" direction, then detonate a charge where two pipes joined. The blast would break the tension, allow the upper pipe to spin free, and allow us to pull up the salvageable sections of pipe.

Success was predicated on getting the explosive charge placed precisely where the two pipes joined. We began by using an explosive "cord" wrapped around a metal probe. But we didn't get it positioned right, and the charge was ineffective when we remotely detonated it deep underground.

---

we didn't **know** we had the measurements **wrong**

Of course, we didn't know we had the measurements wrong. That thought never came to mind.

"Looks like we need a bigger charge," someone said.

"Yeah, let's double it," someone added.

So we did.

We sent down a larger charge of explosive, but the pipe remained stuck—because we were unknowingly discharging the explosives in the middle of a piece of pipe with a wall that was several inches of solid steel.

This further failure resulted in a dangerous, escalating condition that psychiatrists have dubbed the "seven-guys-who-refuse-to-measure-twice-but-who-have-access-to-enormous-amounts-of-dynamite" syndrome.

After about a dozen fruitless attempts, with ever increasing amounts of explosive being shoved into a tube that had a finite diameter, we finally reached the point where we couldn't physically pack any more explosive down the pipe.

(At this point, female readers of this book are thinking, *And it never occurred to you that maybe you could have measured it wrong?* This question simply underscores why drilling for steam is not a career path dominated by women. With that kind of defeatist thinking, we would never have reached the point where we had a fairly reasonable excuse to order up a huge dose of nitroglycerin. Who wants to fiddle with picky little pansy measurements when you can employ enough nitro to blast a crater the size of Minnesota?)

So we found ourselves gathered at the end of an explosives supply truck as a detonation expert fiddled with the nitro.

Someone had to carry the aluminum tube of nitroglycerin up the stairs leading to the deck of the drilling rig. And this someone somehow ended up being me.

They told me it was safe. They also told me to be careful. And to not sneeze. Then they handed me the tube and scampered away.

"Why me?" I said.

"You're single," someone replied.

"But you just said it was safe!" I retorted.

"You'll be fine," they answered. "Most likely. As long as nothing happens. And watch those stairs, they got mud on 'em."

So I carried the nitro up the stairs, sweating like a member of the police bomb squad.

Although we used a VERY substantial charge of nitro, we still hadn't addressed the fundamental problem. We were discharging the bomb in the wrong place. Without placing the charge at the joining of two pipes, we couldn't have blown that thing apart unless we resorted to thermonuclear weapons. Regrettably, the Pentagon gets testy when civilians try to use nuclear weapons, even if you have a perfectly good reason.

The nitro had no effect. So we eventually decided to entertain the possibility of perhaps confirming the location of the charge. (And women accuse men of being stubborn. Bah!) Once we finally discovered our error, we were able to resolve the problem with only a small blast.

Even though the episode ended as a success (with success defined as "Dave lost none of his limbs or internal organs"), I decided right then and there I wasn't going to stay in that job even though the pay was great. Because even without the nitro episodes, I knew I didn't want to be a "roughneck" on a rig. I wanted to be a writer.

I'd always wanted to write. It was in my blood, right next to the plasma and the corpuscles and molecules of Snickers bars.

There's nothing wrong with drilling for steam for a living. It's productive work, and it creates a remarkably clean form of energy. There's nothing wrong with any honest job. But if you have a choice, I believe you should love what you do.

If you *don't* enjoy your job, I suggest you prayerfully consider making a change. Talk it over with your spouse. Seek advice. Probe possibilities. It's so easy to let life happen to us, when we often have far more options than we realize.

And one last piece of advice. If someone starts to hand you a tube of nitroglycerin and asks you to walk up some stairs, begin sneezing. They'll quickly find someone else.

The Worst of Both Worlds

Like many health-conscious Americans, I get an annual physical examination wherein my doctor gives me valuable advice about moderating my diet and exercising more, after which I go have a cheeseburger and fries to celebrate the fact I'm not dead yet.

As I've returned to my doctor year after year, he has become more and more testy and outspoken about how clearly I've ignored all his advice and expertise, as demonstrated by the fact that each new office visit provides him with an opportunity to examine five more pounds of me.

"Dave, you're thirty pounds overweight. Are you exercising at all?"

"I'm walking more, just like you told me," I offered.

"How much more?" he pressed. Doctors are appallingly pushy. I mean, we hand *money* to these people, and rather than show gratitude, they criticize, poke, and prod us.

"Well," I answered him, "the soda machine at the office got moved a few feet so I've added several steps per day."

He wasn't impressed. I think he's simply been brainwashed by the news media. You've probably noticed how tirelessly they've pumped up the topic of obesity in recent years. *Time* magazine devoted most of an issue to the question, "Why Is the Average American Fanny the Size of a Piano?"

But rather than simply blaming readers for their bad eating habits and lack of physical activity, researchers note that basic human biology plays a big fat role. For most of human history, food scarcity has been the rule. God designed our bodies to store fat as a defense mechanism against famine. But with the advent of extremely efficient agriculture in the past century, food is plentiful and cheap. And it tastes better than ever, largely due to the invention of Krispy Kreme donuts.

Because of changing technology, most of us have occupations that don't require us to even break a sweat, much less actually perform difficult manual tasks. In my job, the most physically taxing activity of my day is adding paper to the photocopier. In not-so-ancient times, most people had to engage in demanding physical activity just to stay alive. Plowing fields and churning butter burns way more calories than anything you do in an office, even if you count the aerobic activity of furiously whacking your computer with a stapler when your hard drive crashes.

it's the CUrse of millions

Obesity was once the mark of the idle rich. Now it's the curse of millions.

For many people, food has a significant psychological component to it. People feel bad and then eat to make themselves feel better, in much the same way alcoholics drink to feel better. But even taking the psychology out, dieting is just plain hard. It's hard because the split second we feel pangs of hunger, our body fears we're in a famine and we get this powerful impulse to eat. My body not only fears famine, it fears that someone else is buying the last pint of Ben and Jerry's "Cherry Garcia" ice cream. So my stomach cells override my brain cells, and the next thing I know I'm standing in the frozen food section of my local grocery store while waving a big club and snarling threats at other shoppers.

The standard low-fat diet offers you small amounts of moderately tolerable food, such as reduced flavor cottage cheese and skinless breast of chicken, while offering you unlimited amounts of food you hate, such as parsley, birch bark, and stone-ground celery leaves.

It's therefore no big surprise that most people have failed most of their diet efforts. That is, until the low-carb craze hit.

I first learned about low-carb diets from a TV guy who chronicled how he easily and quite happily shed dozens of pounds while eating loads of foods I always assumed were completely forbidden to any serious dieter. Bacon and eggs for breakfast. A huge chef's salad for lunch, loaded up with meats and cheeses and high-fat dressing. An enormous barbecued rib-eye steak for dinner, paired with a big Caesar salad—minus only the croutons. Inasmuch as I've never been a crouton fan, this news was music to my ears. And once I learned I NEVER had to be hungry, I was actually looking forward to dieting.

I asked my doctor what he thought.

"In your case, my main interest is having you drop the weight. If low carb works for you, fine. Just stick with something and lose the weight. And start exercising!"

I couldn't believe the good news. My doctor had just authorized me to have steak every night. Steak for breakfast, if I wanted. Even steak for dessert!

What could possibly be better?

I went home and explained the diet to my wife.

"It doesn't sound healthy," Dale said. "What about fruits and vegetables?"

"Fruits and vegetables are EVIL!" I warned her. "All those times we had squash and spinach and grapefruit we were KILLING ourselves with wicked carbohydrates! It's amazing we didn't keel over from toxic low-fat yogurt poisoning! Now, let's have a big slab of healthy red meat."

Dale was reluctant, but inasmuch as my doctor had approved, she went along with it.

The results were amazing. I ate like a king for a week, and dropped a pound a day. Sure, I was a little burned out on steak after a solid week of it, but there were all kinds of meat options to try.

In the second week, I dropped another five pounds. I was giddy with low-carb glee.

On week three I had to travel with a colleague named Eric, and we were eating in restaurants quite a bit. I ordered a plate of meat, then went to wash my hands. When I returned to the table Eric was just diving in to the biggest platter of deep fried onion rings I'd ever seen in my life. And he was having a burger. Not a mere burger patty, but a real full-fledged burger with buns made out of *bread*. Not whole-wheat bread either, but bread made out of white, fiber-free, highly processed flour. And he had a side of fries.

"Great food," he said.

"Don't talk to me, you vile little carb toad," I snapped.

"What?" he asked.

"I would trade one of my internal organs for a burger on a bun, fries, and onion rings," I snapped.

"Oh, that's right. You're doing that low-carb thing. Man, I couldn't do that. Gotta have my onion rings," he replied.

"Move to another table, or I'm filing a hostile work environment complaint," I barked.

I scarcely refrained from maiming him with a platter of salami slices.

It wasn't until I returned home, facing yet another plate of fried eggs and greasy bacon, that I had an epiphany.

"Dale! I've solved it!" I said.

"Solved what?" she asked.

"You know how I've been a little cranky lately?" I said.

"You mean like when you told everyone in your office building that if they dared to make a bag of popcorn, you would hurl their microwave oven into the river?"

"Exactly," I replied. "This diet has been grating on me because it's so restrictive. But what if I combined the best aspects of the meat-intensive low-carb diet with, for example, the USDA food pyramid, which includes breads and grains and pastas and fruits and vegetables?"

Dale frowned.

"That sounds suspiciously like no diet at all."

"the diet without **limits**" would be a **bestseller**

"That's the genius of it!" I replied. "I can even patent it as 'The Diet Without Limits.' It'll be a bestseller. I'll be rich!"

"Dave, the supermarket tabloids feature something called 'The Ice Cream Diet,'" Dale said. "They claim you can lose weight by eating nothing but ice cream. Why don't you add that to your 'best of all diets' and then every single dietary boundary will be gone?"

"Wow. Good advice. We'll sell millions!" I said.

"The only downside," Dale mused, "is that anyone who follows your so-called 'diet' will turn into a blimp, have a heart attack, and die."

She quickly vetoed my diet book idea, got some expert advice from a cardiologist, and started feeding us a healthy mix of lean meats, vegetables, and high fiber. We started cooking with olive oil, got rid of the sugar, and only rarely "cheated" with a dessert. We started taking regular walks. And we lost weight.

Every bit as lethal as my "mix and match" diet is the common practice of "mix and match" religion. I occasionally meet people who decide to combine what they see as the "best" of various world religions. So the exclusive claims of Jesus get mixed into a stew of New Age, Buddhist, Islamic, and Native American beliefs. The result is akin to blending a wide variety of mutually contradictory diets until the result is no coherent diet at all.

That isn't a prescription for spiritual health. It's a recipe for soul suicide.

A mix-and-match faith is really no faith at all.

Are You In?

A Christian guy recently took a big risk and confided to me that he has been fighting a losing battle with Internet pornography. He asked me if I would be his accountability partner.

Because of his honesty and sincerity, I felt there was only one answer I could give him.

"No."

I turned him down flat. But I did make a counter offer.

"I'll never be your accountability partner, but I would be honored to be your fellow soldier. I'll watch your back, and I need you to watch mine. I'll be your brother warrior as we fight this gargantuan spiritual battle. But the first thing we're going to do is scrap the whole idea of an accountability partner. It makes me picture myself in my doctor's office, naked, bending over while he says, 'Time for your accountability exam! Cough twice!'"

i am a **flawed** man who's **trying**

I explained that since the Bible never uses the term "accountability partner," I didn't think we needed to use it either. "I'm not your accountant or your electronic monitoring device," I said. "I'm a flawed man who's trying to follow Jesus, just like you. I'm not going to lecture you or judge you. But I'll bear your burden when it gets too heavy, and I'll count on you to do the same for me."

I continued: "A soldier in battle doesn't need an accountability partner. He needs another soldier to fight with him. Two guys watching out for each other stand a far better chance of survival. And a cohesive, committed unit of guys does not merely survive; they pool their courage and skill and bring the fight to the enemy. I want to prevail, not just survive. Do we have a deal?"

"Deal!" he said.

So I don't have an accountability partner. I have a courageous fellow warrior who's kicking some demon butt for the kingdom of God.

And we need reinforcements.

Are you in?

42

Just in Time, or Just What Time?

The alarm clock beeped its irritating greeting at 6:30 a.m. I yawned, stretched, took a quick shower, shaved, combed my hair, brushed my teeth, threw on my sweatpants, and moseyed into the kitchen to start the coffee maker. I glanced at the kitchen clock, which read…6:30 a.m.!

I blinked. Apparently, I'd entered some weird time/space hiccup theorized by Albert Einstein. Either that, or someone had been messing with the clocks.

I phoned the "time" operator and listened to a recorded voice explain that, at the sound of the tone, the time would be 6:23 a.m. and ten seconds. *Both* clocks were off.

I searched the house and discovered that every single one of our clocks was wrong. Every one of them! I stomped into the bathroom as Dale was drying her hair.

"Dale," I fumed, "did you know that *all* of our clocks are set incorrectly? I could have slept another fifteen minutes!" I grabbed the alarm clock to reset it.

"Don't touch the clocks," Dale said.

"But they're all wrong," I protested.

"I have them all set so I can be on time," she replied.

She went on to explain that she set the bedroom clock fifteen minutes fast so she had a buffer if she ran late. The mantle clock in the living room was set ten minutes fast to give her "transition time." She set the kitchen clock five minutes ahead so she had extra time to savor her coffee. Even her car clock was set one minute fast so she had at least one extra minute to walk into work.

"Got it?" she asked, as though this practice was utterly reasonable.

"Let's try another concept," I countered. "Why don't we just set all the clocks correctly, then get up earlier if we need more time?"

"Because when the clocks were set right, I kept running late. It helps me be on time if I think it's later than it really is," she said.

I closed my eyes and rubbed my temples. "Hon, this would sort of make sense—just barely—if it was something *I* did for you, without you knowing about it. But how can those clocks possibly make you think it's later than it is when you yourself set them to be wrong?"

Dale sighed her "let me try to explain this one more time" sigh. "When I see the bedroom clock," she explained, "it makes me kind of panic because I'm behind, so I go faster—but then I have the benefit of knowing I *really* have an extra fifteen minutes. It's the best of both worlds."

I frowned. "This is irrational! It's loony-bin talk! It's complete and utter non—"

"Don't touch the clocks," she cautioned me, as she put on her makeup.

I complained. I protested. I objected. I argued, debated, reasoned, and eventually begged. She didn't budge.

"You'll get used to it," she said.

i felt trapped in a world of make-believe

But I didn't. I felt trapped in a world of make-believe, where we had to pretend what time it is.

If she was in the shower and called out, "What time is it?" I wasn't allowed to glance at my watch and give her the answer. I had to give her the counterfeit time from the bedroom clock. If she was grabbing her purse in the hall, and asked me for the time, I had to specify whether I was giving her the fake time from the kitchen clock or the fake time from the clock on the mantle.

"I'll see you at lunch time," she said as she walked out the door.

"Would that be Pacific Time, Eastern Time, Alice in Wonderland Time, or random 'pick a number out of the hat' time?" I asked.

"Love ya!" she said, blowing me a kiss.

I'm doomed to living in a house without a single accurate timepiece. But, for some utterly inexplicable reason, I've found that both Dale and I are on time more often now than we were back in the days when we set clocks correctly. Weird. By extrapolation of that reasoning, I told Dale I could lose weight faster simply by resetting the bathroom scales, but she just rolled her eyes and told me not to be ridiculous. Go figure.

When it comes right down to it, most of us operate in a make-believe world when it comes to time. Even if we know exactly what time it is, and even if we're prompt and efficient and use day-planners and Palm Pilots, we have no idea how much time is actually left to us. We make plans based on an assumption that today is not our last day, or this month is not our last month. And indeed, we have to make these practical assumptions in order to live and plan in a rational manner. But unless we're careful, there's a certain ungodly audacity that colors the way we view time.

That's why the Bible cautions us against arrogance when it comes to the time left to us:

Now listen, you who say, "Today or tomorrow we will
go to this or that city, spend a year there, carry on
business and make money." Why, you do not even
know what will happen tomorrow. What is your life?

You are a mist that appears for a little while and then vanishes. Instead, you ought to say, "If it is the Lord's will, we will live and do this or that." As it is, you boast and brag. All such boasting is evil.

JAMES 4:13–16

So what time is it—really?

It's time to wise up. It's time to be busy in the activities that matter for eternity. It's time to serve God, to serve our family, to love our fellow human beings, to preach the gospel, and to store up treasures in heaven.

"Teach us to number our days aright, that we may gain a heart of wisdom" (Psalm 90:12).

43

Mistaken Identity

Everyone botches my name. Even people who should really get it right, even people who employ a staff of copy editors to double-check all the details, even major publishing organizations routinely botch my name.

My name is Dave Meurer. That's M-E-U-R-E-R. It is not: Muir, Maurer, Muer, Muerer, Mercer, Moyer, Miller, Merkowitz, or Mephibosheth. I used to get frustrated, but now I'm merely resigned and defeated and stoic and utterly bereft of hope. People will always fracture my name.

A couple of years ago a very nice thing happened to me. In the life of any writer, getting a favorable review from *Publishers Weekly* is a big deal. *Publishers Weekly* is a hugely influential and important magazine that reports on, and shapes, the book industry. Their opinion matters. So when my publicist let me know *Publishers Weekly* had written some laudatory comments about my latest book, I was thrilled beyond words.

Then I saw the review.

They botched my name.

My brief moment of literary glory, my first major favorable book review, and they'd botched my name.

---

professional **boxers** get used to taking it on the **chin**

Oh well. It wasn't exactly a new experience. If you never get punched in the face, the experience can be rather traumatic when it finally happens. But professional boxers get used to taking it on the chin. They don't like it, but it isn't a big shock when it occurs.

I'm not the only one in my family who faces this ongoing issue. My two sons have been plagued by the same problem.

When Mark was graduating from eighth grade, he knew—he just *knew*—that when he walked across the stage to get his diploma, the principal was going to slaughter his name. So he sought her out in advance and gave her the correct pronunciation, making her repeat it back to ensure she really got it.

"I just wanted to have it done right, one time in my life, in a public event," he said.

As the familiar notes of "Pomp and Circumstance" played in the background, Mark walked across the stage as the principal announced, "Mark Nathanael Meer."

The photographer snapped the shutter and forever captured the moment. It isn't just another photo of a happy student accepting his hard-earned diploma. It's a photo of an unsmiling student in the middle of saying, "It's *MEURER!*"

But as much as I'm fussing about this issue, no one in our family suffers as much as my poor wife, Dale.

All through her school years she had to endure questions like, "What kind of name is that? Isn't that a boy's name?"

And that was from the teachers. The kids were even worse.

My wife was named after Dale Evans, the wife and co-star of TV cowboy personality Roy Rogers. (My wife's parents liked Dale Evans a LOT.)

The problem is that the name Dale is overwhelmingly given to males. But there are a few women on the planet named Dale, just like there are a small number of guys named Ashley. (I think Dale got the better deal.)

"Did you say 'Gail?'" Dale has been asked about sixty billion times.

"No, I said 'Dale,'" she'll reply.

"Like, with a *D*?" the person will ask.

"Yes."

"Oh. That's an, um, interesting name," the person will say. "Was your dad named Dale?"

"I was named after Dale Evans," my wife will reply.

If the person is less than fifty years old, this answer prompts a blank stare.

Compounding the confusion, Dale's middle name is Karin.

Not Karen, but Karin (pronounced as in, "Put the *car in* the garage"). It's a Scandinavian name. It's also her mother's first name. Dale's mom grew up having people forever call her Karen, and she had to be forever correcting them. She apparently found the experience so enjoyable she wanted to pass on the tradition to her daughter.

Here's a common scenario in the life of my wife: She walks into our bank to cash a check made out to her. The teller stares at the check and says, "I'm sorry, he'll have to endorse it."

"It's my check," Dale says.

"But Dale needs to endorse the back of it," the teller replies.

"I'm Dale," Dale replies.

"Your name is Dale?" the teller asks.

"Yes. I'm named after a famous woman who was also named Dale, and she rode horses and sang songs on television, and now she's dead."

"Oh," says the teller. "How nice."

At least with me it's only my last name that confuses people. Dale gets it on her first, her middle, and (now that she married me) her last.

But when I married Dale, I also married into the confusion surrounding her first name. I was applying for a credit card over the phone, and here's how the conversation went.

ME: "I would like to open a joint account."

CREDIT CARD GUY: "First and last name of the primary cardholder?"

ME: "Dave Meurer."

CREDIT CARD GUY: "Name of other account holder?"

ME: "Dale Meurer."

CREDIT CARD GUY: "Is this your father, son, or brother?"

ME: "Wife."

CREDIT CARD GUY: (Long pause.) "Is that what he calls himself? Hey, I'm not trying to, like, judge you or anything, but we have all these rules and I think there's a bunch of legal stuff involved and—"

ME: "Dale is a woman."

CREDIT CARD GUY: "Oh. Dale isn't a dude?"

ME: "She's a woman of the female gender."

CREDIT CARD GUY: "Sorry. Okay. Let's complete the rest of the application, Mr. Mohair."

I think it's because my own name has been so abused and twisted over the years that I've developed a habit of playing with other people's names. I routinely give people odd nicknames, often based on a tweak of their real name.

I worked for many years with a guy named Phil Midling. One day I just flipped some letters and started calling him Mel Phidling.

"Hey Mel. Swell morning, is it not?" is a standard greeting I would extend to him.

I called him Mel for weeks, then months, and over time other colleagues began calling him Mel as well. Resistance was futile. The new name had been assimilated.

One day my boss picked up the phone and the caller asked to speak to Phil.

"Hmmm. We don't have a Phil. Did you mean Mel?" asked my boss.

The caller replied, "Well, I have a letter here from your office and it says to contact Phil Midling."

Awkward pause.

"Can I put you on hold for just a moment?" my boss asked.

---

i found her at her desk, laughing so hard she could barely speak

---

She buzzed me on the intercom and told me to get into her office. I found her at her desk, tears streaming down her cheeks, laughing so hard she could barely speak.

"Look what you've done to me! I don't even know the name of my own staff anymore! YOU get to answer the phone and explain that PHIL is away from his desk for a moment but PHIL will call him right back! I can't talk to this guy again after I told him we only had a MEL, not a PHIL. He'll think I'm a blithering idiot," she said.

I recently got an e-mail from a colleague who was venting about the manner in which his name gets killed. "Dude," he said, "look at the way this guy slaughtered my name. I know it shouldn't be a big deal to me, but it is. He always writes 'Derreck' instead of Derek. How hard can it be to get it right? I mean, my name is right there in my e-mail address. He has to spell it right to send me an e-mail, then he spells it wrong in the message. Ticks me off!"

We want people to get our name right, because our name is inextricably linked to our identity. People don't give their children numbers; they give them names. I'm not Human Unit #45672B. Although the Social Security Administration has assigned a number to me, and so has the Department of Motor Vehicles, and so have a bunch of credit card companies, I don't go by a number in my day-to-day relationships. I go by Dave. Dave Meurer. That's who I am.

And that's why I want people to get it right.

I take heart in a touching passage from the Old Testament, where God declares to His people, "Fear not, for I have redeemed you; I have called you by name, you are mine" (Isaiah 43:1 ESV).

I have called you by name.

He knows who I am.

We're sometimes tempted to think of God as so lofty that He sees us as a mass of humanity, not as individuals. But here He is, calling us by name.

Indeed, Jesus said God is so intimately interested in us that He's counted the hairs on our head. The One who really matters most in the universe *knows who you are!*

God gets it right...even when *Publishers Weekly* doesn't.

44
The Naked Truth

Although the situation requires some explanation, there's a perfectly good reason why I was in a women's bathroom. And naked. With another guy. Who was also naked.

For the record, I'd discussed with the other guy the option of our taking turns being naked in the women's bathroom, but he pointed out, quite correctly, that we simply didn't have enough time. But once we finally hit upon the strategy of yelling at each other, the plan made perfect sense (in a stupid sort of way).

The setting was the dormitory at a popular Christian conference center. As my roommate and I wandered down the hall to the restroom on the first morning of the conference, we saw a line of other guys waiting for the showers.

"Looks like we'll be a bit late for breakfast," I said.

"Looks like we'll miss it completely," he replied.

After waiting fifteen minutes, we were the last two guys still waiting in line.

My roommate's head suddenly snapped up. "Hey!"

"Yeah?" I replied.

"This entire floor has been set aside for men during the conference! The women are all on the lower floor. We could use the women's showers on this floor."

I frowned.

"Wouldn't that be, um, well, weird?"

"Nah," he said. "There's nothing sacred about plumbing. We have this entire floor to ourselves. It would be stupid to wait for showers when there are empty ones right here."

"Well, I suppose we could take turns standing guard at the door," I mused.

"We only have seven minutes left to get in for breakfast!" he said.

I hesitated for just a moment, then nodded. "Seize the day!" I affirmed.

We hurried over to the women's facility—and paused at the threshold.

We stared at the "Women" sign on the door.

My roommate took a deep breath.

"All we're doing is using a shower. There isn't anything intrinsically weird about this," he said.

"Agreed. We'll simply be two naked guys in a women's restroom. What could be more normal than that?" I said.

"Exactly," he said, opening the door. "After you."

"Oh, please be my guest," I replied, feeling suddenly polite.

"No," he said, "I insist."

We stood there for a few minutes, being deferential and thoughtful and spiritual and willing to be last, just like the Bible tells us.

We finally entered at more or less the same time.

We halfway expected alarms and sirens and perhaps even peals of thunder and angels bearing flaming swords, but nothing happened. So we proceeded to shed our clothes.

We were in the middle of our showers when my roommate shouted, "Great Scott!"

"What?" I barked, looking wildly around.

"What if the women downstairs suddenly realize there's an unused restroom on this floor? What if they decide to come up here?"

"They wouldn't dare! This is the men's floor!" I replied.

"But they have no reason to think we're in here!" he exclaimed. "It makes perfect sense for them to come up here, in hordes, any second now! And they'll see us, and scream—and call the cops! The press may come! We could be on TV! What will we tell our families? It'll be a nightmare!"

The full implication hit both of us at the same moment.

"We could miss breakfast!" we shouted in unison.

"Think of something!" I roared.

"We need to talk! Loudly! We need to keep up a loud banter so any woman coming to the door will hear us and not come in!" he shouted.

"Good plan!" I yelled back. "How about those Dallas Cowboys?"

"Great team! Very manly sport, football is!"

---

we were simply two **manly** naked men discussing **football**

"Agreed!" I agreed, loudly. "We're simply two manly naked men who happen to be in the women's restroom while discussing football! This is completely normal, and we are *not* lunatics who need to be imprisoned!"

"Absolutely," bellowed my new friend. "This is *not* unusual! I plan to make it a habit!"

"You WHAT!?" I shrieked.

"I mean, I'll *never* do this again! Ever! I'm in the women's showers only because, um, this other guy thought it was a good idea! I'm here under duress! I demand to speak to my attorney!"

I don't remember the rest of the conversation, but it was filled with panic, recriminations, and random sports statistics.

It was years before I whomped up the courage to tell my wife about this traumatic event. She held my hand and listened intently until the end, then collapsed into a heap and laughed until she was left gasping for air like a beached sea bass.

Her show of sympathy was underwhelming.

Even if you've never had a similarly frightening experience, most people eventually have a bad dream in which they find themselves in some public place—the bank, the mall, the church parking lot—completely undressed. It's always a nightmare.

But it could come true. Indeed, unless we take precautions, it *will* come true.

"Nothing in all creation is hidden from God's sight. Everything is uncovered and laid bare before the eyes of him to whom we must give account" (Hebrews 4:13).

All humanity will one day stand before God. You'll either be naked and ashamed, or, in the poetic language of Paul, you may "clothe yourselves with the Lord Jesus Christ" (Romans 13:14).

It will either be a nightmare, or a wonderful dream come true.

Choose.

The Twelve Days of Panic

When it comes to establishing a festive holiday mood, I think nothing beats scurrying through the mall two days before Christmas while hurling random wads of cash at the store clerks and begging them for last minute gift ideas.

As an added benefit, I get lots of excellent cardiovascular exercise as I lunge from store to store in a mad frenzy to finish my list before the mall security guy warns me that the stores are closing in three minutes, and no, I cannot buy his flashlight and handcuffs no matter how cool a gift they would make.

One year I dashed to the counter of the Toys 'R Plastic store moments before it closed.

"I need a couple of those six-wheeled remote-control cars that were in your ad, preferably in red and blue," I said to the clerk.

"Dude, we sold out of those three weeks ago," he replied.

"How about the Mutant Penguin Teenage Robot action figures?"

"Way gone," he said.

"The Jurassic Kid-Eating Bedtime Buddies?"

"On backorder," he said.

"The Video Stupor Gaming System?"

"On backorder *forever*," he said. "Hey, sorry, but I gotta close up the store."

I threw my arms around the closest thing to me.

"How about this big gray object that has blinking numbers and makes noise? It looks fun," I said.

"Um, that's our cash register," replied the clerk.

"I'll throw in five bucks if you wrap it," I said.

I don't know why I choose to put off shopping until the last minute. I think it has something to do with the fact that, given the choice between shopping and having my spleen removed, I'd let them operate.

Basically, I fear stores. I worked for ten years in retail, and on the first day of each November I had to begin stocking the shelves with a hundred cubic yards of Christmas objects while I listened to overhead music playing the same twelve songs over and over and over again until I had all the cheerful holiday spirit of Attila the Hun.

I even found myself changing the words of "Chestnuts roasting on an open fire" to "Santa running as we open fire."

I therefore get all sweaty and twitchy when I even think about going into a store, so I tend to put it off until I'm out of options and in a raw panic.

Dale, on the other hand, prefers to make strategic purchases throughout the year. She buys things on sale, sticks to a budget, and generally acts like a normal adult person. She has also been known to create handmade gifts that the recipients treasure for decades.

One year she asked me, "Why don't you try making some gifts?"

"Because if I tried, it would look like the work of vandals," I replied. "Besides, if God intended us to make gifts by hand he wouldn't have given us VISA cards."

Dale pressed the point. "Dave, Christmas doesn't have to be a horrible shopping ordeal for you every year. And it doesn't have to be extremely expensive. You get in such a panic that you miss the whole point of it. You keep making yourself and everyone else miserable. Why don't you try something different this year? Buy some lumber and make the kids a tree fort. They would love it."

I cringed. I have a couple of brothers who are excellent

carpenters and who can make almost anything. Hand them a bunch of two-by-fours and some power tools, and they could probably build a working Volvo. I, on the other hand, am subject to a court restraining order forbidding me from getting within fifty feet of a jigsaw, lest I pose an unreasonable risk to the neighbors, area pets, and any migratory waterfowl that may be passing overhead.

But Dale was right. The kids would love it. They could use it again and again, and it would inspire their imagination and sense of play far more than some battery-operated fad gift. With proper care and caution, I figured even I could pull off a project like this. After all, we writers may be bookish and clumsy, but we aren't completely incompetent.

So I went downtown and bought plywood, nails, two-by-fours, rope, Band-Aids, antiseptic, tourniquets, and a massive accidental injury policy.

I had no idea quite what to do, but I figured it needed a floor, so I started there. I crisscrossed two-by-fours in the crotch of an old walnut tree and by the time I finished, I still had my arms, legs, and internal organs. So progress was, by definition, good.

The rest of the project just sort of fell into place. By the time I finished I was looking at a cool tree fort that looked a lot like something to top the mast of a pirate ship.

I brought Dale out to survey my work.

"It's perfect," she beamed, giving me a big hug.

"And I didn't maim myself or anyone else," I noted with pride.

Regrettably, the kids weren't the only people on my shopping list. I still had nieces, nephews, parents, in-laws, my spouse, and other assorted relatives. And this meant shopping.

"You still have a week, so you don't have to stress," Dale said. "Try to actually enjoy it. Remember, this is about getting gifts for people we *love*. So don't do your typical thing of buying the first thing you see."

"I like to be efficient," I protested. "It doesn't really matter what you get someone as long as you get them *something*. They can always return it if they don't like it."

Dale rolled her eyes.

"Christmas is a time for *thoughtfulness*," she said. "Last year you ran into Sears like a madman and bought a car battery for our nephew."

"So what's wrong with a practical gift?" I replied defensively.

"Dave, he's six years old!"

"He'll be driving someday," I replied.

I always know when I've scored a logic point with Dale, because she gets an involuntary twitch in her left eye and sends me on an errand. "Why don't you run to the store and pick up a few things for me?" she asked. "We're almost out of milk. And please take the boys so they can keep an eye on you."

"You mean, so I can keep an eye on them," I corrected.

"That too," Dale said.

So I herded the boys into the car and we schlepped off to the supermarket. I was planning to make it a fast trip, but when the boys ventured into the Christmas decoration aisle and saw how inexpensive it was to buy a strand of three hundred miniature lights, they quickly realized we could bring home enough sets to completely cover our windows, hedges, roofline, fence, rain gutters, flower beds, individual blades of grass, and any stray cats that wandered into the front yard.

Plus, it occurred to me that putting up lights would be a nice distraction from shopping.

Dale gasped as we walked in the door with enough lights to illuminate Argentina.

"Why on earth did you buy all those lights?"

"They were on sale," I said.

"But we don't need that many lights," she said. "It's an absurd amount."

"Um, maybe we can give some of them as gifts," I replied. "I bet our nephew could hook them up to his car battery and light up half the city."

Dale heaved a sigh and folded her apron.

"Dave, let's talk. You get so weird around Christmas. What gets into you?"

"What do you mean?" I asked. "Just because I bought a few extra lights?"

"It isn't that," she said. "It's your whole orientation going into the season. I can watch it happen every year. I know that you know that Christmas is really about God sending His Son to earth. Intellectually you know about peace on earth and goodwill toward men. It's supposed to be a great time for celebrating together with family. But you get grouchy and edgy, and you seem to buy into the whole Madison Avenue mindset, like Christmas is all about a shopping list. What's going on in your mind?"

I started to defend myself, but the words died in my throat.

Although God regularly gives us wisdom and insight through the Bible, sometimes He just decides to reach us through our spouse.

As Dale looked me in the eye, I realized I was, in fact,

behaving like an uptight idiot. I was allowing Christmas to get redefined by the most crass and commercialistic notions of the marketplace.

"I'm sorry," I said. "I really don't know what gets into me. You know how I loathe stores, and I dislike shopping. So this season just exacerbates all the things I don't like. Without even thinking about it, I get caught up in the urgency of plowing through a list of names. I know I bring a lot of this on myself by putting things off. And each year I promise myself I won't let it happen again. But, I keep blowing it."

we added in a dose of bona fide ministry

Talking things out with Dale gave me a new sense of perspective. And we also worked out a strategy. She would shop with me, helping me navigate the myriad of stores and the teeming sea of shopping humanity. Plus, we added in a dose of bona fide ministry. We would buy gifts for poor kids overseas as part of a worldwide outreach our church supported.

And thus it came to pass that I, the man who set the American Medical Association's national standard for Holiday Consumer Stupidity Attacks, found myself having an absolute blast as we bought an eclectic assortment of small Hot Wheels cars, bubble blow, Nerf balls, toothpaste, soap, and various gifts to be placed in a shoebox and received with stunned bliss by some poor kid in an impoverished part of the globe. And my gift box would include a message about God about the truly great gift He gave to the world two thousand years ago. These gifts would meet real needs, but also create an audience for the gospel.

In a small way, I was facilitating the joy that God is still bringing to the world. And I was loving it.

This mental shift from "obligation" to "opportunity" was huge for me. And the attitude spilled over into the rest of my gift giving. The stores didn't bother me as much. The hunt for gifts became more enjoyable.

There's a reason the Scriptures tell us, "God loves a cheerful giver" (2 Corinthians 9:7). Generosity of spirit, the delight in blessing someone else, the thrill of bringing joy to another—these are the impulses that beat in the heart of God Himself. Small wonder that He delights to see our heart beating in sync with His.

As children of God, we need to let God's giving spirit permeate our hearts, minds, and even our shopping during the Christmas season. It's too easy to allow Madison Avenue to define the holiday for us. I've been there, and it isn't a pleasant place to visit.

For me, incorporating more of God's kind of giving—where you give to someone who cannot possibly give anything back to you—makes the Christmas season immeasurably better.

By the way, our two boys, Mark and Brad, absolutely loved their tree fort. Their feet barely touched the earth for a week. That was more than a decade ago, and they still talk about it. A personal gift, something from your own hands, can be a great way to make Christmas more meaningful and memorable.

I would try to replicate that success, but I don't think my in-laws would enjoy a tree fort. If, however, they ever decide they would like a shoebox full of bubble blow and toothpaste, boy, am I set!

46

Bob Bob Bobbing to Glory?

As a youngster I was transported in a car that featured two stat-uettes: a head-bobbing puppy in the back window and a plastic representation of the Virgin Mary gazing serenely from the dashboard.

It took some inventive soul forty years to combine those two concepts into the novel figurine that's on the market today—a bobbing-head Jesus.

When Solomon penned the immortal words, "There is a time for everything under heaven," somehow I don't think he had this in mind.

I don't know which fact is worse—that bobbing-head Jesus dolls exist, or that people are purchasing them.

Generically speaking, bobbing-head dolls are either amus-ing or stupid, depending on your point of view. But they're *never* reverent.

Now, I have nothing against bobbing-head dolls per se. I actually own one. My doll's gently bobbing head features a photo of my book editor. Whenever my editor does something outrageous or immoral, such as actually editing any of my words when they were *perfectly fine* just the way they were, I can whack him upside his tiny little head and watch him quiver. It's a fulfilling experience, and one of the most uplifting highlights of my day.

But it's one thing to mock an editor, and an entirely dif-ferent thing to trivialize God. If a bobbing-head Jesus isn't outright mockery, it's skating dangerously close.

I really, really, really hope these idiotic items don't start turning up in Christian bookstores, but I'm not betting the farm on it. After all, many Christian bookstores already feature hideous quantities of "Jesus Junk." A case in point: the Christianized mints commonly found by the cash register of religious stores.

Unlike the pagan "Certs" or heathen "Tic-Tacs," the Christianized mints have a cross stamped on them. The theory is apparently that if the unbelieving masses observe Christians gobbling up mints with crosses imprinted on them, a nationwide revival will take place, multitudes of sinners will repent, angels will rejoice, and the "holy kiss" Saint Paul talked about will take on a whole new meaning.

While I'm not a big fan of Jesus Mints, a friend of mine named Charlie Jones is wild about them. He thinks we need a whole assortment of Christianized mints we can share with the unrepentant. He suggests "BanishMints," "ChastiseMints" and even "JudgeMints," perhaps stamped with little flames.

I was delighted when the Jesus Mints finally vanished from the counter of my local bookstore. But within a few weeks there was a replacement. I picked up a cellophane wrapped tin, looked at the cover, and shuddered. Whereas your average godless Philistine grocery store carries Altoids, your average Bible bookstore is now featuring "Almighty Mints," packaged with the following quote:

> The Spirit of God has made me; the *breath* of the
> Almighty gives me life.
>
> JOB CHAPTER 33, VERSE 4

"You've GOT to be kidding," I said to the store manager.

"Um, people buy them," she offered in defense.

"This is the most awful commercialization of the faith I've ever seen," I complained.

"Oh, you haven't seen anything," replied the manager.

"What could be worse?"

"Well, the WWJD wristbands started to slack off in sales, so we're recycling them," she said.

"Recycling?" I asked, puzzled.

what **would** Jabez do?

"Since the letters are the same, we're marketing them as 'What Would Jabez Do?' bands," she whispered.

"No!" I gasped.

"Just kidding," she replied.

Frankly, it wouldn't have been all that surprising.

If this trend keeps up, I fully expect to see a line of Christian sandals ("Walk like Jesus walked!"), Christian cell phones ("Talk like Jesus talked!"), Christian sunglasses ("See with the eyes of faith!"), and Christian mascara ("Look like Mary Magdalene looked until she converted!").

We're already halfway there. Many Christian "bookstores" are crammed with far more trinkets than books. And these trinkets, baubles, stickers, posters, rings, pens, glass angels, shirts, socks, and ceramic salt shakers with "Ye are the salt of the earth" written on them in tiny cursive script have become de facto substitutes for the nitty-gritty task of actually sharing the gospel.

Meanwhile another promoter has produced "Christian" nylons with tiny crosses stitched into them. But the apostle Paul warned sternly against the danger of taking away what he called the "offense of the cross" (Galatians 5:11). The cross was not amusing. It wasn't a joke. It was God's extremely serious answer to our extremely serious need for redemption.

Jesus Mints do not save souls, and bobbing-head Jesus dolls do not honor the Messiah.

I expect the world to mock God, but I expect better behavior out of believers. So I'll continue to harangue my local Christian bookstore to get rid of "Jesus Junk."

Maybe I'll create my own line of HarassMints.

47

This Town Sucks!

As we motored along an Arkansas freeway, I looked at the sign and blinked, not quite believing what I was seeing.

"They have a town called Toad Suck?" I asked my friend, Tim.

"Yep," he replied.

"Why would any community decide to call itself a revolting term like Toad Suck?"

Tim shrugged. "Maybe some other town had dibs on Salamander Suck."

"Do you think their ancestors actually sucked on toads?" I gasped.

"I've always been partial to frogs, myself," Tim responded.

"Har dee har. Remind me again where you're taking me," I asked him, "and why I agreed to come."

"We're going hiking in beautiful Petit Jean State Park, and you agreed to come because we've been friends thirty years, and this is a great opportunity to catch up on our friendship and enjoy God's creation."

"Fair enough. But if anyone offers me anything unnatural to eat, I'm outta here," I warned him.

We arrived at the park and decided to have dinner at a nice restaurant overlooking an expansive valley. The food was quite good and, happily, quite toadless. Greatly relieved, I asked the waitress about dessert.

---

their **specialty**, she said, was deep **fried** cheesecake

"Well, our specialty is deep-fried cheesecake," she said.

I burst into a merry fit of laughter and, once I gained my composure, wiped the tears of mirth from my eyes and asked, "But seriously, what do you have?"

"She isn't joking," Tim whispered.

I was stunned.

"How in the world can you deep-fry cheesecake?" I asked.

Picking up on my Yankee accent, she quickly decided I wasn't being rude, but simply dense.

"Well, we take a cheesecake," she said slowly, so I could

follow along. "And then we deep-fry it."

Wouldn't *that* just clot your corpuscles!

Arkansas was definitely *not* home.

But come to think of it, even my hometown isn't my home. The Bible says we're strangers in this world. We *should* feel out of place, especially when it comes to the appetites and desires of a world system that's contrary to God. The fare the world offers us—envy, jealousy, pride, lust, hate—is far more dangerous than a truckload of fried cheesecake. Or even sucking on toads.

48

Close Calls and
Mysterious Mercies

For an exciting Fourth of July celebration, nothing beats the combination of friends and family, homemade ice cream, and a wayward mortar round exploding right above your head and raining down big clumps of flaming debris.

We were sitting on the lawn at a city park, crowded in among twenty thousand other residents of our town, "oohing" and "ahhing" as the fireworks show exploded overhead. Typically, we would hear the tell-tale "whump" of the projectile being launched, followed by the dazzling explosion a few seconds later. But one of the shells detonated prematurely as it left the firing tube, spraying sparks at ground level.

There was literally no time to react. And even if the crowd

had wanted to run for cover, we were crammed together like little sardines. By the time my brain registered the danger, a flaming, hissing green blob of errant firework was streaking through the sky on a direct trajectory for my left nostril.

Quickly gathering my wits, I managed to sit there and yell "GAAAAAHHHHHH!"

A puff of summer breeze intervened, and the burning remnant landed about ten feet in front of me—right smack in the middle of the only unoccupied patch of lawn within several square acres. It was amazing no one was hurt. The crowd closed in for a better look at the burned grass, and a TV reporter lugged a camera to the scene to record the near miss.

It seems like life is full of close calls, near misses, and barely avoided disasters. Was this near miss the specific intervention of God?

Dale pondered that possibility aloud. "It's odd that no one had their blanket laid out there, in the only available space around. I mean, look at all the wall-to-wall people everywhere else. Why was no one in that exact spot?"

The same thought had crossed my mind. Was it a mysterious mercy? Did God intervene?

But what about those times when disaster is not averted? What about the times when a drunk driver plows into the innocent pedestrian, or cancer turns malignant? Why does God allow that? Where is the guardian angel when the child gets seriously wounded in an accident?

We don't know. We can't know, at least this side of heaven. What we *do* know, whether our circumstances turn out great (Daniel gets delivered from the lion's den) or awful (Stephen gets stoned to death), is that God loves us. God is good, even when circumstances are bad.

We can drive ourselves crazy trying to second-guess or make sense out of the providence of God. I've seen people lose their faith by trying to figure out why God allowed a certain Bad Thing to happen. They equated suffering with abandonment, and they decided God was either a cosmic sociopath or nonexistent. On more than one occasion I've come dangerously close to joining them. Suffering can truly shake us.

We delight in deliverance. We're heartened when our prayers get answered. We're grateful for the good times. All these good things can strengthen our faith.

But faith is also forged in the crucible of distress, disaster, and suffering. And the Bible makes it glaringly clear that God in His wisdom is willing to allow His children to go through troubled waters as He goes about his *unceasing* work of conforming us to the image of Christ.

extraordinary victories as well as unspeakable suffering

Indeed, in the eleventh chapter of Hebrews (the Bible's "Hall of Faith"), we read a jumble of extraordinary victories as well as unspeakable suffering.

We're reminded here of the heroes "who through faith conquered kingdoms…who shut the mouths of lions, quenched the fury of the flames, and escaped the edge of the sword; whose weakness was turned to strength; and who became powerful in battle and routed foreign armies" (Hebrews 11:33–34).

But read on:

> Others were tortured and refused to be released, so
> that they might gain a better resurrection. Some faced
> jeers and flogging, while still others were chained and
> put in prison…. They went about in sheepskins and
> goatskins, destitute, persecuted and mistreated—the
> world was not worthy of them.
>
> HEBREWS 11:35–38

God never takes responsibility for evil, even though He permits evil. And He's willing to use evil for His own purposes. When Judas sold out Jesus, it was an act of deep treachery and staggering evil. And the Bible never excuses it. Yet the evil of Judas was used by God to bring about the divine plan of salvation. It was foretold in the Old Testament; it was all part of the plan. We must embrace both these facts, though there's no way we can explain the dichotomy.

God's character is unimpeachable, and we dare not assault His holiness or His goodness by maligning His nature or His motivations. But we also need to come to grips with the fact that He often permits and utilizes calamity and woe.

I've heard some theologians try to dodge the conundrum by saying God is "doing the best He can." That's utter nonsense. It lowers God to the status of a well-intentioned but completely overwhelmed deity—a divine juggler who keeps dropping one or more of the balls. You might pity a god like that, but you certainly wouldn't stand in awe of him. And you would be a fool to trust him.

We can't explain the unexplainable. We're mortal, we're

limited, and we're not going to be able to figure out God. We can understand quite a bit, but never all. Not in our mortal state.

Faith is mature and vibrant when we, like Job, can say, "Though he slay me, yet will I trust in him" (Job 13:15 KJV).

If a raw chunk of rock could make sounds while the master craftsman cut it into a valuable diamond, I think we would hear a steady string of "ouch!" noises. But the result is glorious.

God knows what God is doing, even if we don't. This needs to be enough for us.

And when it *is* enough—then that, I believe, is a huge part of what faith is all about.

Technically Speaking...

My doctor asked me to take a seat as we reviewed the results of my recent blood test.

"On the plus side, you don't have cancer," he said.

I was stunned. "Did you think I had cancer?"

"No," he said. "The lab accidentally checked you for it anyway, so I figured I would start off with the only good news in the entire batch of dismal results."

"But I feel great," I protested.

He folded his arms and got that irritated look he typically gets when I show up in his office having clearly ignored his last lecture about my sedentary lifestyle. "Dave, do you realize that every time your annual physical rolls around I examine five more pounds of you?"

"I like to think of myself as the gift that keeps on giving," I said.

"I think of you as a candidate for a stroke," he said. "All your test results are worse than last time."

"Isn't there *any* good news?" I asked.

He glanced at the chart.

"Well, you don't have scurvy and you aren't pregnant. But that's the end of the good news. Your bad cholesterol is high, your good cholesterol is low, your stomach diameter puts you only an eighth of an inch away from an official risk factor, and your blood sugar level is high. That last one has me especially concerned."

"Why?" I said, biting my lip.

"Because your blood sugar count has never been this high before," he said. "But if it's that high in two consecutive tests, then by definition you're considered a diabetic. And if you're diabetic, I basically become your drug pusher, and you'll be on several different medications the rest of your life."

I winced.

"Dave, we've had serious talks for years. You leave my office promising to make changes. But then you lapse into your old habits."

this guy was a **broken** record

I knew what was coming next. That same old lecture about diet and exercise. The guy was a broken record.

What I really wanted wasn't a lecture, but some pills that would essentially negate the logical consequences of my bad habits.

"Did you remember," asked the doctor, "to fast for twelve hours before your blood test?"

I nodded.

"So, no food after eight 8:00 p.m.?" he asked.

"Well, I might have had just a small nibble of pie, but certainly nothing like I normally have for dessert. But back to—"

"YOU are going to have another blood test in three days. NO FOOD FOR TWELVE HOURS! Is that clear?" he asked, getting that hoity-toity "I know better than you on account of I went to medical school" tone of superiority.

I decided to comply. After all, I *had* put on a few more pounds than I wanted to. According to the guidelines of the American Medical Association, my height and weight put me in the category of "large Chevy sedan."

So I ate exactly what I was supposed to eat, and I walked every day for thirty minutes. The day after my test, I called the doctor's office and got his nurse on the phone.

"Well, Mr. Meurer, your blood sugar level is down. It still isn't good, but you aren't yet a diabetic."

I breathed a huge sigh of relief.

"Any further questions I can answer for you today?" she asked

"Well, in light of the good news, can I safely go and celebrate with a burger, shake, and fries?"

There was a long pause.

"Please," she said, "tell me you're not serious."

"What I mean is, technically, I could keep the good food coming just as long as my blood sugar doesn't test too high. Right?"

She huffed. "Ask a worthless question, you get a worthless answer."

"What?"

"Mr. Meurer," she explained, "the question isn't some legalistic argument about whether you're officially a medical basket case yet. The question is, What can you do every day to move closer to health and further away from your dangerous inclinations? You sound like a teenager who's playing word games with his youth pastor about how far he can go with his girlfriend before he's 'officially' crossed the line. If you keep asking that question, you're heading for disaster."

She continued, "Now, do you want to do the right thing? Or shall I inform the doctor of our little chat and also schedule your next prostate exam? Trust me; he can make it *very* unpleasant if he's in a bad mood."

"Um, I have to go now," I said. "It's time for my morning walk, which I'll take in a lively and aerobic manner."

SPECIAL NOTE TO TEENAGERS: You can learn a lot from your elders. For example, this little story teaches you that I'm capable of being an idiot. So learn something. Ask the right questions. And don't get technical with God.

God loves you…but He's not a fool.

All Washed Up!

It wasn't a design flaw. The amount of shelf space built into our prefabricated shower stall is perfectly suitable for a bar of soap, a bottle of shampoo, and a bottle of conditioner. The problem is that the shower was obviously designed by a guy who wasn't married. Otherwise he would have known there had to be space for no less than sixteen assorted bottles, jars, soaps, and other permutations of body cleaning products.

I had to buy a triple shelf storage thing to hang on the neck of the showerhead just to begin holding all the bath stuff Dale uses.

When I took my shower this morning, I used exactly two products—a bar of soap and a bottle of shampoo. I was done in five minutes.

Dale never showers in five minutes. It takes longer than that to simply open all the lids she uses.

Here's a partial list of the stuff she has in our shower: a tube of Cucumber Citrus Skin Polish, which the label says is "to exfoliate, moisturize, and buff"; a jar of Mango Body Scrub; a tube of Strawberries and Champagne Cleansing Cream; a bottle of Mango Mandarin Shower Gel; a tube of Moisture Rich Body Lotion; a bottle of Comfrey and Orange Lotion; an Oatmeal & Lavender Facial Bar; a container of some imported pink stuff called "Lait Parfume pour le Corps"; a square-bottled product called "Clinique Dramatically Different Moisturizing Gel" (apparently to distinguish it from the moisturizing gels which are Undramatically the Same); and several French products that, curiously, feature the word *toilet*. (You'll note that not one of these products contains the word *soap*.)

And that's not the end of it. Not by a long shot. Our shower is also lined with different hair care products designed to add body, create fullness, restore bounce, address split ends, counter heat damage, and intensely moisturize. I have to assume at least one of them also actually shampoos.

"Is all this really necessary?" I asked Dale one day.

"Of course," she replied. "That's why I have them."

If we go on a trip, I can easily fit all my bathroom stuff—shampoo, soap, toothbrush, comb, shaver—into a little canvas bag that's smaller than a loaf of bread. If I was packing all Dale's shower and post-shower stuff, I would need a wheelbarrow.

"Why do women *do* all this?" I marveled one day as I stared at all the bottles.

"We do it for ourselves," she replied, "but also for the man in our life."

Oh. Well, that's different then. She should have said so in the first place. These products are a rather stellar idea. They should make more of them.

there remains a **dirty** reality

But no matter how many cleansing items fill our shower, and no matter how much they make us look tidy and smell fresh, there remains a dirty reality. God has looked at us more than skin deep, and He has found unclean hearts. Our spirits have been thoroughly soiled by our sins. And adding to the trouble: We have no ability to scrub away the mess.

That's why King David made this plea to God: "Have mercy on me, O God, according to your unfailing love; according to your great compassion blot out all my transgressions. *Wash away all my iniquity and cleanse me from my sin*" (Psalm 51:1–2).

There's desperation and honesty in that prayer. And it's a prayer God will answer. He said so: "Though your sins are like scarlet, they shall be as white as snow; though they are red as crimson, they shall be like wool" (Isaiah 1:18).

But how? How does a Holy God forgive sins for which justice cries out for punishment?

He does it justly.

God doesn't merely ignore our sins. He doesn't sweep them under a rug or spray some divine air freshener to simply cover up the nasty, reeking reality of our sins.

He did something substantive about our sins. It's hard for language to really capture such a profound spiritual reality, and I think that's why God uses several word pictures to describe what He has done to make it possible for us to be clean and innocent before Him.

In addition to the word picture of washing away our bright red stain, He also uses the analogy of a paying off our crushing, impossibly huge debt. The Bible tells us that when Jesus died on the cross, He was paying this debt for our sin. Someone who had never sinned—the unique Son of God, who shared the very nature of God—paid a ransom for us. That ransom was His *life*.

Afterward, dead and buried, that Someone rose up out of death, proving that the ransom actually worked.

Use whichever word picture helps you best understand what God is trying to communicate—a paid debt, a washed stain, a healed disease. All of them capture the idea. He did for us what we couldn't do for ourselves. And the key thing God requires of us is to believe Him when He says that what Jesus did is truly enough. This is an act of faith, an exercise of trust.

So we put down the scrub brush, and we stop trying to scour away the stain. We stop trying to hide the blotch from His all-seeing eyes. We cease conning ourselves by saying it really isn't all that bad of a stain. No, we admit that the mess is glaring and ugly. The stain of sin utterly penetrates us, and it's completely beyond our ability to wash away.

So we bring the mess to God, at His invitation, and ask Him to please clean it. We humble ourselves before the Almighty. We ask Him to forgive us. We ask Him to clean us up and make us "white as snow"—thereby fit to enter heaven and ready to begin a new life here on earth.

If you've never asked…why not ask right now?